PREHISTORIC ANIMALS
AN A-Z GUIDE

MICHAEL BENTON

Illustrated by
Jim Channell and Kevin Maddison

DERRYDALE BOOKS
New York

First published in 1989 by Kingfisher Books

Copyright © Grisewood & Dempsey Ltd 1989

This edition published by Derrydale Books,
distributed by Crown Publishers, Inc.,
225 Park Avenue South, New York,
New York 10003

Printed and bound in Spain by Gráficas Reunidas, S. A.

ISBN 0-517-69190-6
h g f e d c b a

Front cover: *Mammuthus*
Previous page: *Diadectes*
This page: *Chalicotherium*

CONTENTS

DISCOVERY OF PAST GIANTS

People have collected fossils, the remains of long-dead plants and animals, for years. Indeed, early cave dwellers of 20,000 years ago or more noticed fossil shells in the flints they carved into arrowheads and axes. However, they had no idea why they found perfect shells and other fossils in the rocks. How had they got there?

Much later, quarryworkers in various parts of Europe found particular kinds of fossil shells and bones in the stone they were working. Occasionally, they would show their fossils to scientists, but they were equally puzzled about their meaning. Some even thought the fossils had been planted in the rock by the Devil.

The first large bone to be reported from Europe was part of the leg bone of a dinosaur found near Oxford, England. In his book, the *Natural History of Oxfordshire*, published in 1677, Robert Plot of Oxford University described the bone as that of an elephant or a giant human. He was not very sure of these identifications, but at least he realized

An archaeological dig for a mastodon skeleton. Some bones were reported from a farm in New York state in 1801. Charles Wilson Peale led an expedition, financed by the American Philosophical Society, in 1802, to dig the rest of the skeleton out. Dozens of workers were employed, and water had to be pumped out of the pit to prevent flooding.

that the specimen was a bone.

In 1725, a remarkable fossil skeleton was discovered at Oeningen in Germany. It was sent to Dr. Johann Scheuchzer, the town physician of Zurich, Switzerland, who thought that it represented one of the miserable human sinners who had been killed by Noah's flood. In an illustrated account of the skeleton, published in 1727, Scheuchzer argued that he had been able to prove that the great flood of the Bible had covered Europe and drowned many humans and animals. It was shown later that this skeleton was actually a giant salamander!

Many bones of giant animals came to light during the 1700s. In particular, great fossil elephants, mammoths, and mastodons were discovered in northern Europe and in North America. These had obviously not all been drowned in a single flood. Some scientists argued then that such animals still existed in unexplored parts of the world.

Finally, scientists realized that many of the fossil skeletons they found belonged to extinct animals, that is forms which died out some time ago. Finds of giant bones excited the public and scientists alike, and there was a great campaign to find more. Great excavations were carried out around 1800.

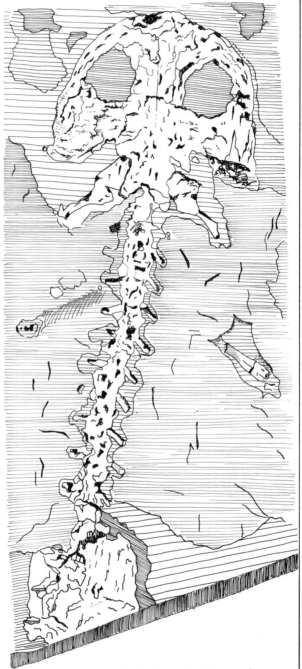

Homo diluvii testis, the fossil salamander found in Germany in 1725, and identified as a human skeleton.

VICTORIAN DISCOVERIES

During the 1800s, the Victorian age, scientists learned a great deal about geology (the study of the history of the earth) and about paleontology (the study of the history of life). Many new fossils were found and it became clear that the earth was millions of years old. During the long history of the earth, hundreds of remarkable prehistoric animals had come and gone.

In the 1820s important finds were made in England. They included the first dinosaurs, *Megalosaurus* and *Iguanodon*, and the first sea dragons which lived at the same time. These sea dragons included the dolphinlike *Ichthyosaurus*, and the long-necked *Plesiosaurus*. Both these dragons were first collected by Mary Anning, a famous early professional collector. One of the leading paleontologists of the day was Baron Georges Cuvier of Paris, who demonstrated how to build up the skeletons of these remarkable extinct animals from scattered bones. He studied fossil reptiles, but particularly various kinds of extinct mammals. Fossils of mammoths and mastodons of the great ice ages seemed increasingly common. Scientists traveled from Europe to poorly known parts of the world, and came back with huge bones of bizarre

Othniel C. Marsh was a professor at Yale College in Connecticut. He studied hundreds of new prehistoric reptiles, mammals, and birds (*Hesperornis* and *Ichthyornis*) which his collectors sent back from the Mid-west.

Edward Cope is famous for the huge number of new species of dinosaurs and fossil mammals which he named and described during his lifetime. For most of this time, his deadly rival was Marsh, and they often disagreed.

Baron Georges Cuvier was the first professional paleontologist to show how to rebuild the skeletons of prehistoric animals from scattered fossil remains. He studied fossil mammals and reptiles from all parts of the world.

The great fossil hunters

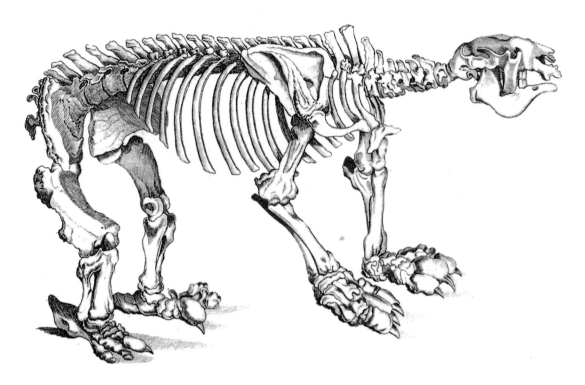

animals. Charles Darwin, the famous "father of evolution," visited South America in the 1830s, and found the huge bones of the great ground sloth, *Megatherium*, and the giant armadillo, *Glyptodon*. Other scientists visited Australia, and found the remains of giant kangaroos and wombats. All of these animals had obviously lived side by side with early humans, but had since died out.

Some of the most important finds were made between 1850 and 1900 in North America. The great paleontologists Edward Cope and Othniel C. Marsh paid for large teams of prospectors to find fossils in the American Mid-west. They uncovered the huge bones of dozens of new

The skeleton of a remarkable prehistoric mammal sent from Argentina to Spain in 1788. It was mounted in a realistic pose, and later described by Georges Cuvier as *Megatherium*. Although it looks like a rhinoceros in size, Cuvier could tell that it was closely related to the modern tree sloth.

species of dinosaurs and mammals. Initially they cooperated but later fell out and became rivals. Their teams often clashed in their efforts to uncover new finds. They found that great tracts of Nebraska, Wyoming, the Dakotas, and Utah yielded a series of all kinds of extinct mammals. Since 1900, our knowledge of prehistoric animals has expanded enormously, and new forms are still found every year.

THE AGE OF THE EARTH

How can scientists tell how old the earth is, and when all of the prehistoric animals lived? This question has puzzled people for centuries. At first, most scientists believed they could work out the age of the earth from the Bible. Indeed, James Ussher, the Archbishop of Armagh in Ireland, calculated that the earth came into being in 4004 B.C., less than 6,000 years ago.

This estimate was accepted by most people in the 1600s and 1700s, but many geologists began to question it. Scientists such as James Hutton could not see how this could be long enough for the earth to reach its present form. He saw how long it took for a river to cut its way down through the rocks.

He asked how the great thicknesses of sandstone and limestone around the coasts of Britain could have formed in 6,000 years, when these rocks were being formed in modern lakes and seas at very slow rates. He argued that the earth was immensely old.

By 1850, most scientists accepted that the earth was very ancient. They could also see that the fossils which they found in the rocks seemed to form a pattern through time. The older fossils in any sequence seemed simpler than the later ones. Older rocks contained only shellfish, then the fish appeared, then amphibians, then reptiles, then mammals, and finally humans in the very youngest rocks.

Far left: Charles Darwin, the most famous scientist of the 1800s, showed that life had evolved over many millions of years from a single common ancestor. His theory of evolution is the basis of modern biology and palaeontology.

Left: James Hutton, an important geologist of the late 1700s. He argued that the Earth must be immensely old in order to allow time for all the complex processes on the surface of the Earth to take place.

From the Bible to Darwin

Charles Darwin made a major contribution in 1859 when he proposed the theory of evolution by natural selection. He argued that all plants and animals, living and extinct, are related to each other, and that they have evolved over millions of years into all the different forms we see about us, and which we can find in the fossil record.

In Darwin's day, geologists could date the rocks by the fossils they contained. The evolution of life meant that rocks of particular ages had specific fossils in them. What is more, in any pile of rocks, the oldest ones were at the bottom, and the youngest ones at the top.

Exact ages in millions of years were only found in the 1900s by the study of radioactivity. Some rocks are radioactive, and it is possible to measure their ages when the rate of radioactive breakdown is known.

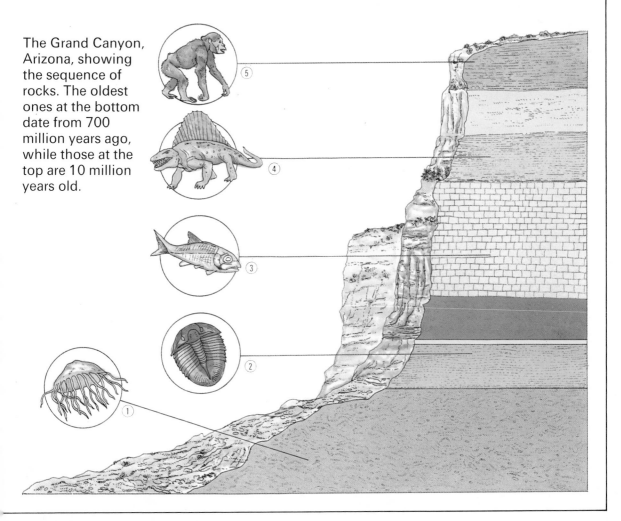

The Grand Canyon, Arizona, showing the sequence of rocks. The oldest ones at the bottom date from 700 million years ago, while those at the top are 10 million years old.

HISTORY OF THE EARTH

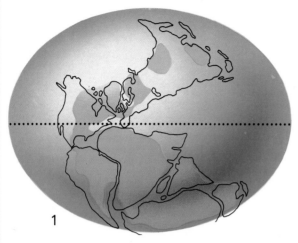

1

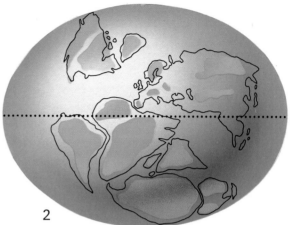

2

Continental drift in action. The changing face of the Earth over the past 400 million years. The maps show how the continents have moved since the Permian (1). The shift northwards had begun by the Cretaceous (2) and by the Palaeocene (3) the continents had broken up further. During the Oligocene (4) the World had begun to look much as it does today. The continents are still moving: Europe and North America move away from each other by half an inch a year.

The present world seems constant and changeless. However, it is not. Even the solid ground beneath your feet is not as solid as it seems. The crust of the earth is actually divided up into a number of great plates which are moving about very slowly. Every year, for example, North America and Europe drift apart by half an inch or so as the Atlantic Ocean becomes wider.

This seems a very slow rate of movement, but over the millions of years of the earth's history great changes have taken place in the layout of the continents and oceans. For example, some 200–100 million years ago, during the age of the dinosaurs,

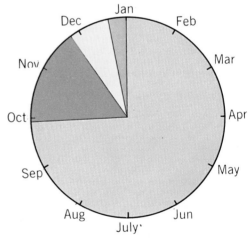

The history of life on Earth represented as the course of a single year. The Earth is about 4600 million years old. First life appeared in late September (3500 million years ago, *red*); moved onto land in November (400 million years ago, *yellow*). Mammals arose in December (245 million years ago, *blue*) and humans began to appear on New Years Eve (5 million years ago).

How the continents were formed

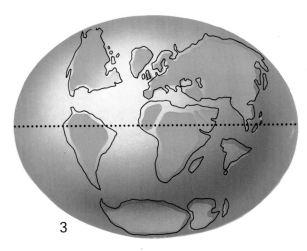

3

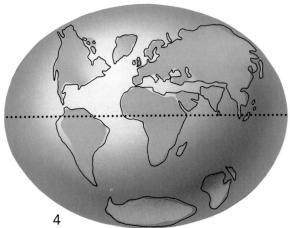

4

all the continents were fused together as one great supercontinent, and land animals could wander freely all over the surface of the earth. Since then, the supercontinent has broken up, and the present Atlantic and Indian Oceans have appeared.

The positions of the continents in the past can be worked out by studying the rocks and fossils. The direction of the ancient North Pole can be found by examining tiny magnetic particles in the rocks. Also, in some cases, a single species of plant or animal is found in rocks of the same age in parts of the world that are now far apart. They could not possibly have traveled to these now disant places and this suggests how the continents used to be arranged. The changing face of the earth has clearly had a great effect on the animals and plants that lived on land in the past.

Lystrosaurus, (*below*) an animal that "proves" continental drift. Skeletons of the same species have been found in South Africa, Antarctica, South America, India, China, and the U.S.S.R. It must have been able to walk overland from place to place, and this was possible because there was only one great supercontinent 245 million years ago.

HOW FOSSILS ARE FORMED

There are many kinds of fossils. The commonest fossils are the remains of shells or bones which have been turned into stone. These show all of the original details of the shell or bone, even when they are examined under the microscope. All of the pores and tiny spaces in their structure have been filled with minerals.

The minerals are chemical compounds like calcite (calcium carbonate) which were dissolved in water. The water passed through the loose sand or mud containing the shells or bones and the minerals were deposited in the spaces. This is why a fossil bone or shell is heavier than a modern one.

Other fossils may have lost all traces of their original structure. For example, a shell made originally from calcite may dissolve completely after it has been buried. It may then be replaced by calcite in another form or some other mineral which forms a perfect replica of the original shell. In other cases, the shell is dissolved away and nothing is left but a hollow space in the rock, a kind of mold of the specimen which can be filled with plaster to show what the animal looked like.

Footprints are a special kind of fossil that can tell us a great deal about the life of extinct animals. These were made by the first humans *Australopithecus*, 3.75 million years ago, when a mother and child walked along together across a layer of ash.

How animals turn to stone

Millions of years ago, an ichthyosaur died and sank to the bottom of the sea. Its body lies there for some time and the flesh decays. Fish and other creatures may feed on the body.

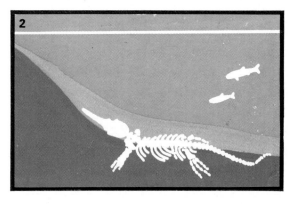

Eventually, only the hard bones are left behind. Layers of sand and mud are washed over the bones of the ichthyosaur and it is buried in the position it lay.

Over millions of years, the skeleton is buried deeper and deeper. The sand and mud turn to rock (sandstone and mudstone) and the bones are filled with minerals, making them into fossils.

Many millions of years later, the seas withdraw and the ancient sea bed is lifted up. The layers above the ichthyosaur skeleton are worn away by wind, rain, and rivers.

Fossils usually show only the hard parts of a plant or animal — the bark of a tree, the shell of a shellfish, or the bones of a fish or dinosaur. Some fossils are much more complete, however. If a plant or animal body is buried in particular kinds of mud which contain no oxygen, the fossils may have soft parts preserved as well. The most spectacular of these "perfect" fossils are woolly mammoths found in frozen soil with their flesh deep-frozen. The meat is so fresh it can still be eaten after 20,000 years!

CLASSIFYING THE FOSSILS

Paleontologists know that the earth is very ancient and that life arose many hundreds of millions of years ago (*see pages 10–11*). They also know that life arose on the earth once only and that all living and extinct plants and animals are related to each other. This means that there is one great evolutionary tree that links all forms of life together and that everything shares a common ancestor that lived 3,500 million years ago.

This may seem quite remarkable when you compare an elephant and a mushroom, a worm and an oak tree. How can they all share the same heritage? The evidence is very strong for this, however. Not only do thousands of fossils tell us the shape of the great tree of life, but all living things share some unusual chemicals

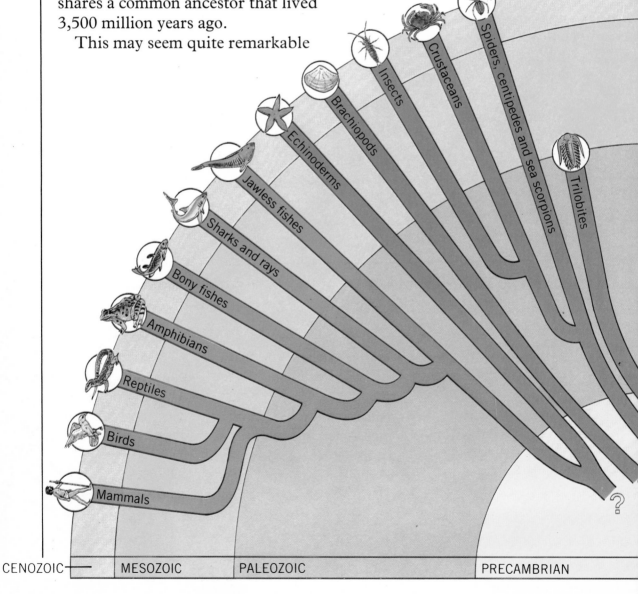

| CENOZOIC | MESOZOIC | PALEOZOIC | PRECAMBRIAN |

The ancestry of living creatures

within their cells that are found nowhere else. So, the elephant and the oak tree, the worm and the mushroom look very different on the outside, but on the inside they share some crucial chemical similarities that prove that they share the same distant ancestor. In the diagram below, the main groups of animals and plants are shown on a time scale of the past 700 million years or so. Scientists know the shape of some parts of the tree quite well, and the lines are joined together. However, there are parts where we cannot say where the links occur, and these are shown with question marks. This book is about the prehistoric animals on the far left of the picture — the fossil amphibians, reptiles, birds, mammals, and humans.

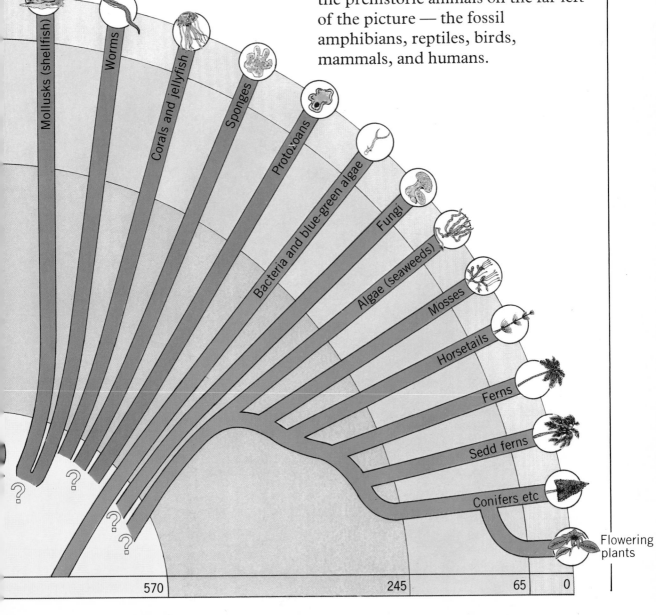

570   245   65   0

THE A–Z INTRODUCTION

The main part of this book is an alphabetical guide to all the important prehistoric animals. Thousands of extinct amphibians, reptiles, birds, and mammals are now known, so the most important ones have been selected. Each major extinct group is represented by at least one animal. The dinosaurs are not included in this book, since there are so many of them, but all the other groups that lived during the age of the dinosaurs are shown. All the important dinosaurs may be found in *Dinosaurs: An A–Z Guide*. Most of the names are from Latin or Greek words which tell you something about the animal — how big it was, or what it ate, for example. Under the name of each

prehistoric animal is a guide to how to say the names, and an explanation of the meaning.

Underneath this is the name of the person who gave each animal its name, and the date that it was given. The country or countries where skeletons have been found is given next, and the age of the prehistoric animal is given and also shown on the pictorial time scale to the side (*see key below*).

The silhouette shows the outline shape of each animal and the size relative to a bone hunter 5 foot 9 inches tall. The length is given in feet below. The color of the animal tells you to which major group it belongs (*see color guide below*).

> Pronunciation guide
? What the name means
ⓝ Who named the animal and when
① Where the animal was found
◆ When the animal lived

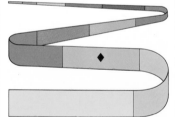

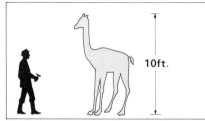

10ft.

* Million years ago

Devonian	408*	Paleocene	66
Carboniferous	360	Eocene	55
Permian	286	Oligocene	37
Triassic	245	Miocene	25
Jurassic	208	Pliocene	5
Cretaceous	144	Pleistocene	2

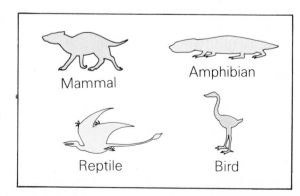

Mammal

Amphibian

Reptile

Bird

Classifying *Homo sapiens*

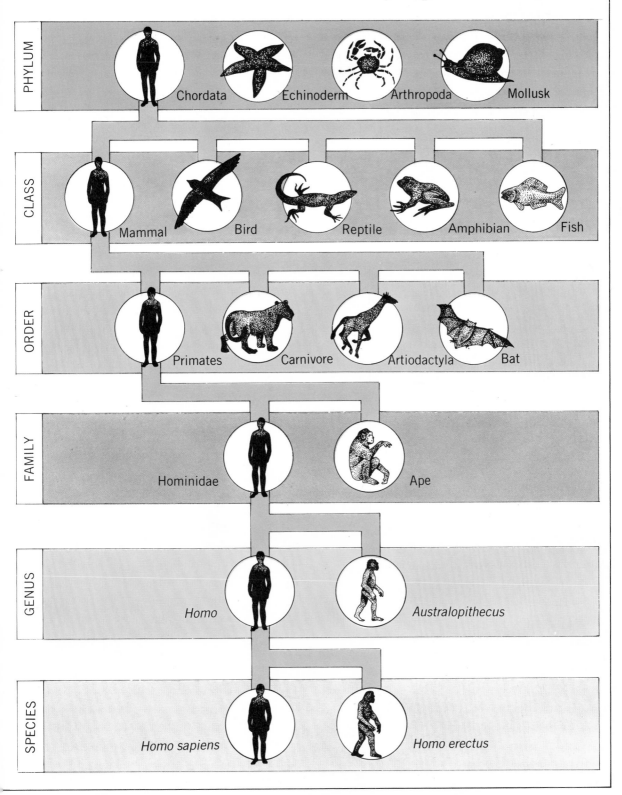

AEGYPTOPITHECUS

> ee-JIP-toe-PITH-e-kus
? Egyptian monkey
ⓝ E. L. Simons (1965)
ⓛ Egypt
◆ Oligocene

1½ft.

Since we are human beings, it is only natural that we want to identify our oldest ancestors. *Aegyptopithecus* is close to being the oldest known ape, and thus the missing link between apes and humans on the one hand, and monkeys on the other. This small animal is known from partial skulls and odd bones of the skeleton from Egypt in rocks dating back 30 million years. The head and body of *Aegyptopithecus* are monkeylike in appearance, and it probably ran about on all fours along stout branches. The apelike teeth suggest that it ate fruit, a highly nutritious source of food. *Aegyptopithecus* is thought to be close to the origin of the apes because it has a braincase which is larger than that of a monkey, and apelike teeth.

ALLODESMUS

> AL-oh-DES-mus
? Other chain
ⓝ R. Kellog (1922)
ⓛ California Oregon Japan
◆ Miocene

6ft.

The seals and sealions are unusual groups of meat-eating mammals that live largely in the sea feeding on fish. It is known that they arose from land-living meat-eaters, but their early evolution is uncertain. *Allodesmus*, one of the oldest sealions, had large eyes which were probably important for hunting fish underwater. Its ears were probably not so well developed as in modern forms which use their acute hearing to pick up the slightest movements in the water. *Allodesmus* was clearly a swimmer since its hands and feet were modified into broad paddles.

ALTICAMELUS

> AL-tih-CAM-eh-lus
? Tall camel
ⓝ W. D. Matthew (1924)
ⓛ California Nebraska
  Texas
◆ Miocene

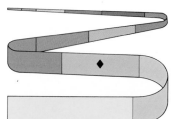

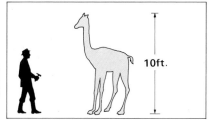

10ft.

At first sight, *Alticamelus* looks like a strange mixture of a deer and a giraffe. However it is a camel, and one of a great variety of fossil camels that lived in North America from 30 to 5 million years ago. It was only after then that the camels moved into South America, Asia, and Africa, where they now survive. The early camels like *Alticamelus* probably lived on large grassy plains, feeding on grass and leaves, in rather desertlike conditions, as today. *Alticamelus* had a long neck so that it could feed on leaves high in bushes and trees which other plant-eaters could not reach.

Alticamelus

EVOLUTION OF THE AMPHIBIANS

The amphibians were the first vertebrates (animals with backbones) to walk on the land. They arose from fishes during the Devonian period, some 380 million years ago. At that time, other forms of life had just conquered the land. The first plants, insects and worms moved on to the land about 420 million years ago. Until that time, all plants and animals seem to have lived in the sea. The earth must have seemed very strange with no green plants and no moving things on land.

During the Devonian, many groups of fishes lived in the seas and in great warm lakes. From time to time these lakes dried out, and certain groups of fishes evolved ways of surviving in these new, dry conditions. They were able to breathe the air using primitive lungs, and they had strong fins that could be used to pull themselves across the mud and into a pond that still contained water. Today, some groups like the lungfishes and the catfishes can breathe air for a short time, and also drag themselves about out of the water.

The amphibians probably arose from some Devonian fishes that behaved rather like modern lungfishes. Life out of the water was difficult at first. The air dried the skin and there was no longer any water to support the weight of the body or to hide in. However, the temptations of a life on land were great, too. There were plenty of succulent worms, spiders and millipedes moving about in the plants at the water's edge. The first amphibian, *Ichthyostega*, had plenty of food! The amphibians ruled the earth during the Carboniferous period, 360–286 million years ago. Some, including *Crassigyrinus*, *Greererpeton*, and *Megalocephalus* remained close to the water and fed

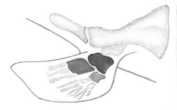

The three main bones in the fin of a Devonian fish. This configuration developed into the leg shown to the right.

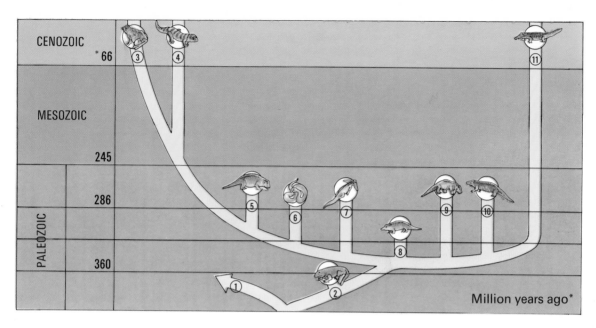

| | | Million years ago* |

CENOZOIC
*66

MESOZOIC

245

286

PALEOZOIC

360

on fish. Others, such as the later *Eryops, Limnoscelis,* and *Seymouria* became adapted to living on dry land, and they probably fed entirely on land animals while others like *Ophiderpeton* lost their legs and lived like aquatic snakes. These primitive amphibians gave rise to the modern amphibians, frogs, and salamanders, 200 million years ago.

Key to amphibian evolution

1 Fishes
2 Ichthyostega
3 Frogs
4 Salamanders
5 Eryops
6 Ophiderpeton
7 Diplocaulus
8 Megalocephalus
9 Seymouria
10 Diadactes
11 Reptiles

The bones in the leg of *Ichthyostega* have developed in such a way that the animal can support itself on land.

ANDREWSARCHUS

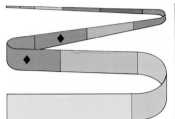

> AN-drew-SARK-us
? Andrew's ruler
ⓝ H. F. Osborn (1924)
① Mongolia
◆ Eocene Oligocene

15ft.

Andrewsarchus was probably one of the most terrifying meat-eaters of all time. Its skull is 3 feet long, four or five times the size of the largest living lion or tiger. In life *Andrewsarchus* probably looked like a giant horse-sized hyena, although it belongs to an extinct group of mammals that is not closely related to modern dogs or hyenas. It fed by tearing meat from

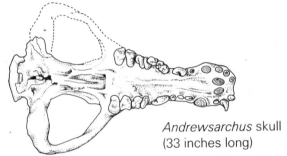

Andrewsarchus skull
(33 inches long)

carcasses using its broad cheek teeth which were adapted for crushing bone.

ANTHRACOTHERIUM

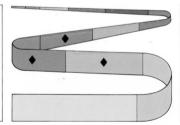

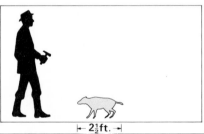

> an-THRAK-oh-THEE-re-
um
? Coal beast
ⓝ F. Cuvier (1822)
① Asia France
◆ Eocene Miocene

2½ft.

Although they look rather different, pigs and hippopotamuses are closely related. The anthracotheres, which are now extinct, may have shown features of both groups since they seem to have lived in or near swamps in warm climates, but also had short legs with cloven hooves for running. *Anthracotherium* has a long skull lined with sharp teeth at the front and broad crushing teeth at the back. It probably fed on a mixed diet of tough plants, roots, and leaves. The sharp front teeth may also have been used to capture animals for food — pigs today can eat a completely mixed diet of plant and animal food. The tusks may have been used in fighting.

ARCHAEOPTERYX

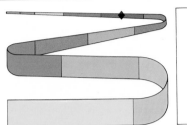

> AR-kee-OP-ter-ix
? Ancient wing
ⓝ R. Owen (1864)
ⓛ Bavaria
◆ Jurassic

1 ft.

Archaeopteryx may well be the most famous fossil animal of all. It is described in nearly every book about the history of life and evolution because it is thought to be a perfect example of a "missing link," between the reptiles and the birds. This means that it shows primitive features of the reptiles, such as teeth, claws on its hand, and a long bony tail, as well as advanced features of the birds, such as feathers and a wishbone. It is the oldest known bird because of the last two characteristics. *Archaeopteryx* could probably have flown about as well as a modern bird, but it is not certain whether it flew from tree to tree, or over the open ground.

The first fossils of *Archaeopteryx* were found in 1861, and since then a total of six skeletons have been found, the last in 1987. They are preserved in a fine limestone which used to be quarried to produce printing plates. The limestone was laid down in a warm lagoon near to land, and it preserves many fossils beautifully: jellyfish, worms, complete fish, flying reptiles with their skin, and *Archaeopteryx*.

Archaeopteryx

ARCHAEOTHERIUM

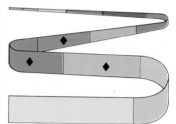

> AR-kee-oh-THEE-ree-um
? Ancient beast
ⓝ J. Leidy (1850)
ⓘ South Dakota
  Nebraska Asia
◆ Eocene Miocene

← 4ft. →

Early in their history, the pigs were much more varied and widespread than they are today. One early group, known from the forests of North America, Europe, and eastern Asia, 25 to 50 million years ago, were the entelodonts such as *Archaeotherium*. These early piglike animals reached lengths of 10 to 13 feet, about the size of a hippopotamus, but they were taller and more agile on land. The skull was very long, and it bore sharp teeth at the front, including a pair of tusks, as well as many broad grinding cheek teeth behind. The jaws are deep, which shows that there must have been powerful jaw muscles. There are also some large bony knobs on the lower jaw, but their function is unknown.

Archaeotherium probably fed on tough plants and roots. The area of the brain involved with the sense of smell was huge so *Archaeotherium* may have been able to sniff out tasty roots underground using its snout. It had a short neck because of the great size of the head: a massive head needs massive neck muscles to move it about. The legs were long enough to allow *Archaeotherium* to run through the woods. The entelodonts died out as great grasslands spread over North America, Europe, and Asia, since they were probably not adapted for life in the open.

Archaeotherium

26

ARCHAEOTHYRIS

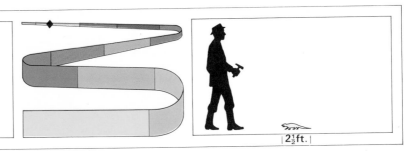

> AR-kee-oh-THY-ris
? Ancient window
ⓝ R. R. Reisz (1972)
① North America
◆ Carboniferous
  Permian

| 2½ft. |

Archaeothyris skeleton

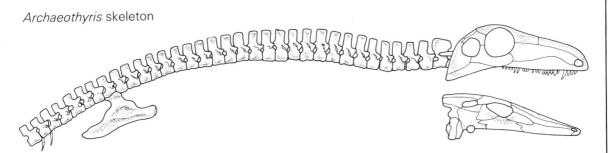

The mammallike reptiles were an important group on land from about 320 to 225 million years ago, one which included most of the plant-eaters and meat-eaters of the time, particularly the larger ones. They are also important because they chart the origin of the mammals from their reptile ancestors.

Archaeothyris is the oldest known mammallike reptile, being represented by a partial skull and skeleton found in a fossilized tree stump in eastern Canada, as was *Hylonomus*.

Archaeothyris was a small animal, and probably looked more like a lizard than a mammal. Its long narrow-snouted skull has a large eye socket, and a single opening behind that. This opening at the back, known as the *temporal fenestra*, probably had

something to do with the attachment of the jaw muscles, but it is important for another reason. All mammals, as well as the mammallike reptiles, show this particular skull pattern, and its presence in *Archaeothyris* identifies it without doubt as the earliest known, and very distant, ancestor of the human race.

The teeth of *Archaeothyris* are pointed and peglike, and they vary in length. These teeth are adapted for piercing the outer shells of beetles and other insects which were common in the warm and wet forests where *Archaeothyris* lived. The skeleton of *Archaeothyris* is not known completely, but it probably had a long tail, and long sprawling limbs which would have allowed it to dart about like a modern-day lizard.

ARCHELON

> ar-KEE-lon
? Ancient turtle
ⓝ Wieland (1896)
Ⓛ Wyoming
◆ Cretaceous

12ft.

Fossil turtles are generally very much like modern turtles. The whole form of the body is controlled by the "shell" that covers the back and the belly. One of the most unusual fossil turtles was *Archelon* which is known from many skeletons in limestone deposits in the ancient shallow seaway that ran down the middle of North America from Alberta to Texas. The giant *Archelon* is a member of an extinct group that shows a reduction of the shell to narrow riblike strips and star-shaped plates. The shell is made from bone in all turtles, and it is fixed to the ribs and other parts of the skeleton. The loss of bone in the shell of *Archelon* may have been to save weight. It was a huge animal, bigger than modern sea turtles, and probably had to be able to swim fast in order to catch fish. The massive paddlelike arms and legs probably drove the body forward by moving in a figure-eight pattern like the paddles of modern turtles.

Archelon

ARCTOCYON

> ARK-toe-KY-on
? Bear tooth
(n) H. D. de Blainville (1841)
(l) North America France Germany
◆ Paleocene

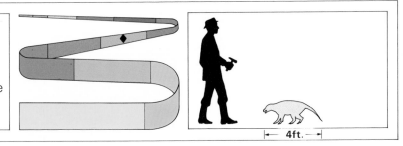

Arctocyon belongs to an extinct group of meat-eating mammals and is probably closer to the large plant-eaters than to modern cats or dogs. This sheep-sized animal had large fangs that would have been used for piercing flesh, but the cheek teeth behind are broad and flat, so more useful for grinding tough plants.

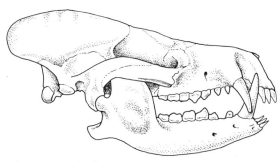

Arctocyon skull

ARDEOSAURUS

> AR-dee-oh SAW-rus
? Burn reptile
(n) H. von Meyer (1860)
(l) Germany
◆ Jurassic

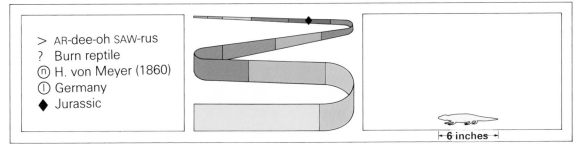

The lizards evolved some 170 million years ago. Although earlier examples have been recorded from time to time, they are of doubtful origin. *Ardeosaurus* is important since it is one of the oldest well-preserved lizards, being known from several nearly complete skeletons. They have been found in fine limestones, just like those containing *Archaeopteryx*, and the tiny bones, including the hairlike ribs, are all present in their correct positions. *Ardeosaurus* is about 6 inches long, and has a broad skull and long sprawling limbs. It is like modern geckos in many respects, and may have lived like them, feeding on insects in poor light.

ARGYROLAGUS

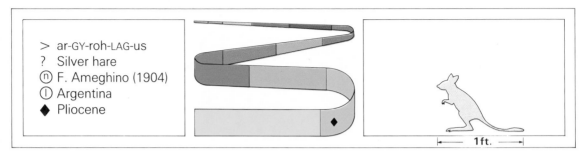

> ar-GY-roh-LAG-us
? Silver hare
ⓝ F. Ameghino (1904)
ⓛ Argentina
◆ Pliocene

⊢—— 1ft. ——⊣

At first sight, *Argyrolagus* must have looked like a rabbit, with its long hind legs, its short arms, and gnawing teeth. It may well have had long rabbitlike ears but these are not preserved in the fossils. However, *Argyrolagus* was part of a remarkable and independent evolution in South America throughout the last 70 million years. Until about three million years ago, South America was an island, and its land life evolved separately from the rest of the world. The marsupials, the pouched mammals, were present in South America, and they took on many of the roles filled by placental mammals elsewhere. The South American marsupials have now nearly all died out. Close relatives of *Argyrolagus* include the catlike *Thylacosmilus* and the bearlike *Borhyaena*.

Argyrolagus

ARSINOITHERIUM

> AR-sin-oy-THEE-ree-um
? Arsinoë's beast
ⓝ H. J. L. Beadnell (1920)
ⓘ Egypt
◆ Oligocene

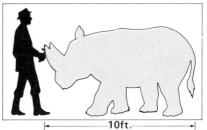

10ft.

One of the oddest fossil mammals must be *Arsinoitherium*, a strange rhinoceroslike animal. It is known from good skulls and skeletons from the same deposits as *Aegyptopithecus* in Egypt and some poorer ones in the Middle East. Its most obvious feature is the pair of huge "horns" that arise above the snout. They are fused at the base, and are hollow inside. In males they have points at the end, but are smaller and round-tipped in females and young animals. In life, these "horns" were covered with skin, which is shown by the presence of blood vessels on the outside of the bone, so that they were probably more like the skin-covered knobs on top of a giraffe's head than the horns of a rhinoceros. *Arsinoitherium* has high teeth which may have been used to grind up tough plant food.

Arsinoitherium

ASKEPTOSAURUS

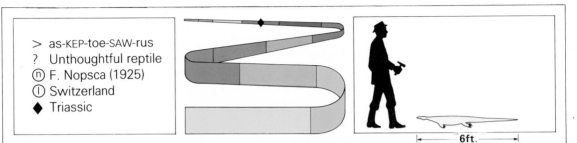

> as-KEP-toe-SAW-rus
? Unthoughtful reptile
ⓝ F. Nopsca (1925)
ⓘ Switzerland
◆ Triassic

6ft.

During the Triassic period (245 to 208 million years ago), many groups of reptiles that had always lived on the land tried out life in the sea. *Askeptosaurus* was a member of a group possibly related to the ancestors of the lizards that entered the sea. The long head was lined with sharp teeth for gripping slippery fish, while the body was enormously long, and almost snakelike. *Askeptosaurus* probably swam by beating its body from side to side, and steered with its paddlelike hands and feet.

Askeptosaurus skeleton (6 feet long)

ASTRAPOTHERIUM

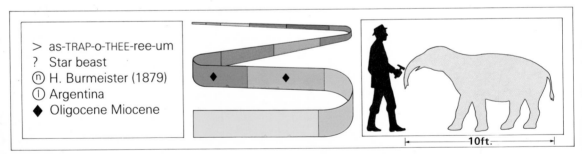

> as-TRAP-o-THEE-ree-um
? Star beast
ⓝ H. Burmeister (1879)
ⓘ Argentina
◆ Oligocene Miocene

10ft.

While the pouched marsupials evolved along many unusual lines in South America (see *Argyrolagus*), some lines of plant-eating placental mammals also became important.

Astrapotherium is a typical example of an extinct group that was important about 20 million years ago. It was as large as a rhinoceros, but had rather short legs. The head is short and there are two large nostrils placed high on the snout which suggests that *Astrapotherium* had a flexible trunk in life. There were two long upper tusks that may have been used to rake up plant material or to chop tough stems.

AUSTRALOPITHECUS

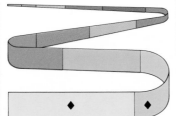

- > o-STRAL-oh-PITH-eh-kus
- ? Southern monkey
- Ⓝ R. Dart (1925)
- Ⓘ Kenya
- ◆ Pliocene Pleistocene

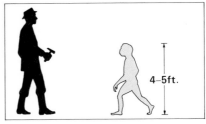

4–5ft.

True human beings, some think, probably evolved about five million years ago, as is indicated from comparisons of modern humans and our nearest relatives, the chimpanzees. The oldest known fossil humans belong to a form called *Australopithecus* which date from nearly four to a million years ago. There were several species, some as light and small as a chimpanzee, and others as tall as a modern human. These all lived in eastern and southern Africa where they searched for plant food (fruits, nuts, and roots) as well as small animals when they could catch them.

    Australopithecus could walk fully upright on their hind legs, just as we can, but they still had an ape-sized brain.

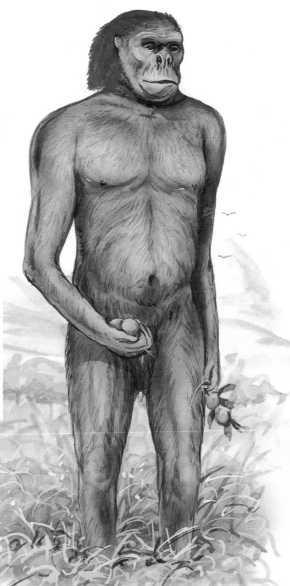

Australopithecus

BARBOUROFELIS

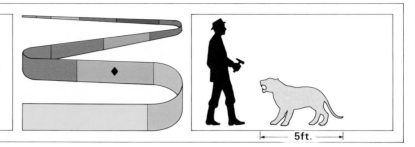

> BAR-bur-oh-FEE-lis
? Barbour's cat
(n) E. H. Barbour and G. H. Cook (1914)
(l) Texas
◆ Miocene

5ft.

Barbourofelis

The largest cats today are the lions and tigers which can capture large deer and antelope by biting through their skin in a weak place. In the past, several groups of cats were able to attack much larger animals, often with very thick skin.

Barbourofelis was a "dirk-toothed" cat, one of a group that had long daggerlike fangs in the upper jaws. It could open its mouth wide and sink the pointed teeth through the skin of an early elephant or rhinoceros. *Barbourofelis* had shorter legs than many modern hunting cats, and was not able to run fast. Although it looks rather like the saber-toothed cat *Smilodon, Barbourofelis* probably evolved its long fangs separately.

BASILOSAURUS

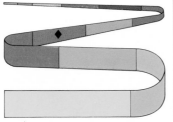

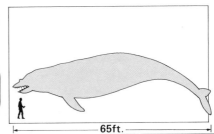

- > BA-zil-oh-SAW-rus
- ? Royal reptile
- ⓝ R. Harlan (1834)
- ① North Africa North America
- ◆ Eocene

65ft.

Whales are mammals and not fish. They are warm-blooded and they bear live young which are fed on milk and come up to the surface of the water to breathe. For a long time the origin of the whales was a mystery. It is known that the whales evolved from land mammals, but the skeletons of *Basilosaurus* gave little idea of how this happened. The recent discovery of an even older whale, *Pakicetus*, has helped. *Basilosaurus* was about 65 feet long, as big as many of the large whales today. Modern whales have large heads, whereas *Basilosaurus* has one that is only 5 feet long. The teeth are pointed and lined with jagged spikes so that it probably fed on fish. *Basilosaurus* swam by sideways movements of its long body, and steered with its broad paddlelike hands. The hind legs were almost completely lost.

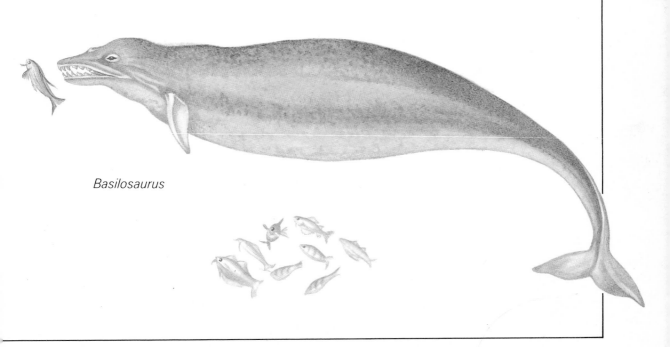

Basilosaurus

EVOLUTION OF THE BIRDS

The first bird, *Archaeopteryx*, flew about over the warm lagoons that covered parts of southern Germany 150 million years ago. The first fossils of this bird were found in 1861, just after the publication of Charles Darwin's *On the Origin of Species*. The evolutionists immediately saw that *Archaeopteryx* was a perfect "missing link," an animal that lies midway between two major groups; in this case the reptiles and the birds. Several complete skeletons of *Archaeopteryx* have been found since 1861, and they are all exceptionally well preserved. They show all of the delicate hollow bones in great detail, and the feathers are even preserved as impressions on the mud. At first, some paleontologists thought that the new specimens were really small dinosaurs, because the skeleton was reptilelike: there was a long, bony tail and the jaws were lined with sharp teeth. The feathers prove that *Archaeopteryx* was the first bird and it seems likely that the birds arose from dinosaurian ancestors some 160 million years ago. During the Cretaceous period (144–66 million years ago), the birds became more modern in appearance. They lost the

The fossil of *Archaeopteryx*, regarded as the "missing link" between reptiles and birds.

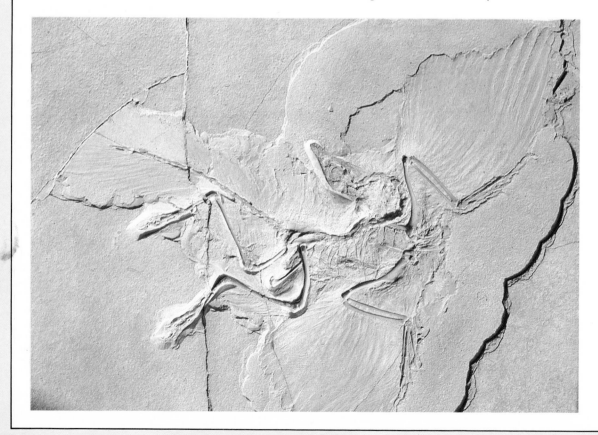

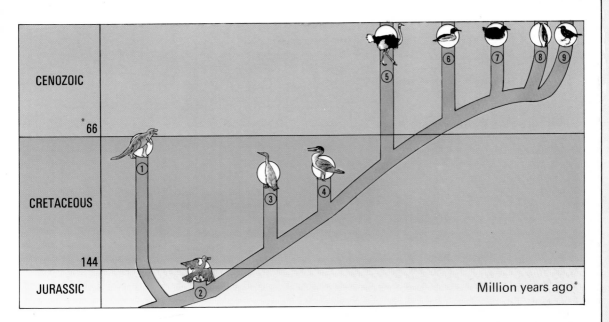

CENOZOIC	
*66	
CRETACEOUS	
144	
JURASSIC	Million years ago*

long bony tail, the claws on their wings and eventually their teeth. However, the best-known Cretaceous birds, *Hesperornis* and *Ichthyornis*, still had teeth which they used for catching and cutting up fish. During the 66 million years of the Cenozoic Era all the modern groups of birds arose. The exact story of their evolution is not very well known because good bird fossils are very rare. Modern birds fall into two main groups, the flightless forms like ostriches, emus, and kiwis, which lost the use of their wings, and the flying birds.

The flying birds seem to fall into two groups. The ducks, geese, hens, and pheasants form one group which seems to have evolved separately from all others. The rest which make up the remaining population are hard to classify precisely.

Key to evolution of the birds

1 Meat-eating dinosaurs
2 Archaeopteryx
3 Hesperornis
4 Icthyornis
5 Ostriches and emus
6 Hens, ducks
7 Shore birds
8 Penguins
9 Perching birds

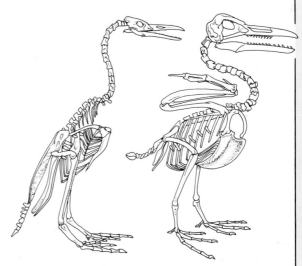

Skeletons of the Cretaceous birds Hesperornis (*left*) and Ichthyornis (*right*).

BORHYAENA

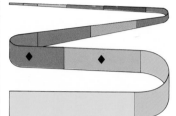
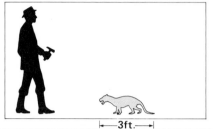

> BOR-hy-EE-na
? Northern hyena
Ⓝ F. Ameghino (1887)
Ⓘ Argentina
◆ Oligocene Miocene

├─3ft.─┤

The South American marsupials were formerly very important as rabbit-mimics (*Argyrolagus*) and as meat-eaters. *Borhyaena* probably looked like a small bear, and it had teeth rather like those of a hyena. The fangs were used for piercing flesh, while some of the cheek teeth could have been used to crush bones. Other relatives ranged in size from that of a fox to a large bear, so that this group was able to feed on a wide range of plant-eating animals.

Borhyaena had short stocky legs and its feet are planted flat on the ground, so that it was probably not a fast runner. The fast-running meat-eaters of that time in South America were large birds, such as *Diatryma* and *Phorusrhacos*.

BRANCHIOSAURUS

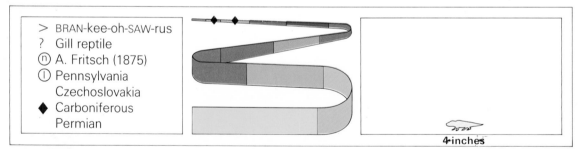

> BRAN-kee-oh-SAW-rus
? Gill reptile
Ⓝ A. Fritsch (1875)
Ⓘ Pennsylvania
Czechoslovakia
◆ Carboniferous
Permian

4 inches

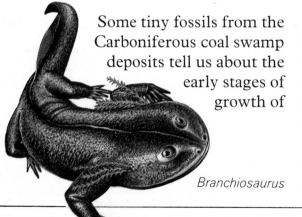

Some tiny fossils from the Carboniferous coal swamp deposits tell us about the early stages of growth of some of the early amphibians. They have large heads, short arms and legs, and large feathery gills for breathing under water. These small animals are all called *Branchiosaurus*, and some of them may be tadpoles of amphibians like *Eogyrinus* or *Eryops*, while others may be adults that just look like tadpoles.

Branchiosaurus

BRONTOTHERIUM

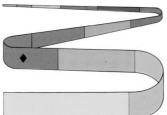

> BRON-toe-THEE-ree-um
? Thunder beast
(n) W. B. Scott and H. F. Osborne (1887)
(l) South Dakota
◆ Oligocene

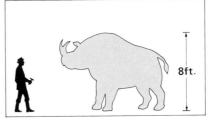

8ft.

The brontotheres were a group of large plant-eaters that looked rather like rhinoceroses, but which are only distantly related to them.

Brontotherium and its relatives fed on leaves from trees and bushes, and they lived generally in the large warm forests that covered North America, Europe, and parts of Asia.

Brontotherium was larger than any living rhinoceros, and it had a remarkable forked "horn" on its snout, shaped rather like a catapult. This "horn" was larger in males than in females, and it was probably used in fighting, just as the horns of deer and antelope are today. The brontotheres died out at a time when their natural forests were being replaced by great grasslands. They were unable to eat the new grasses, and they were replaced by horses, rhinoceroses, and other modern groups which could.

Brontotherium

CAPTORHINUS

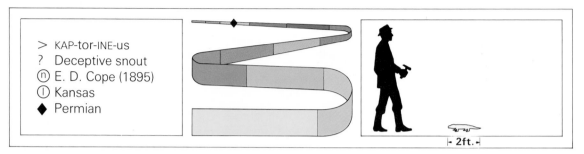

> KAP-tor-INE-us
? Deceptive snout
ⓝ E. D. Cope (1895)
ⓛ Kansas
◆ Permian

- 2ft. -

At the time when sail-backed, mammallike reptiles such as *Dimetrodon* and *Edaphosaurus* dominated the land as medium-sized to large meat-eaters and plant-eaters, *Captorhinus* was an important smaller plant-eater. *Captorhinus* and its relatives probably looked rather like large-headed lizards in life, but they had primitive skulls and other features that show that they were not related to either the mammallike reptiles or the ancestors of the lizards and dinosaurs which were around at the time. They had unique patterns of teeth consisting of more than one row in each jaw. *Captorhinus* had three or four separate rows of teeth across a broad jaw bone used for crushing tough plant material.

CASEA

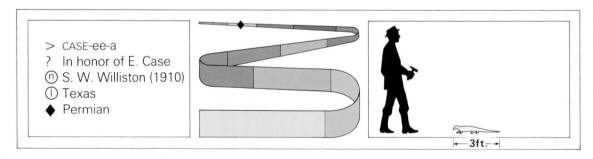

> CASE-ee-a
? In honor of E. Case
ⓝ S. W. Williston (1910)
ⓛ Texas
◆ Permian

— 3ft.—

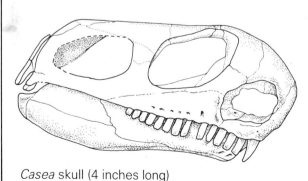

Casea skull (4 inches long)

The first amphibians and reptiles all fed on meat in one form or another: fish, insects, or other amphibians and reptiles. *Casea* belonged to one of the first groups to specialize in plant food. It has a broad skull and its jaws are lined with long blunt teeth used for chopping soft plant stems, as well as a large nostril and eye socket.

CHALICOTHERIUM

> CHAL-i-ko-THEE-ree-um
? Pebble beast
ⓝ J. J. Kaup (1833)
ⓛ Kenya Turkey Spain
◆ Miocene

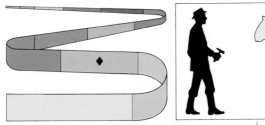

10ft.

One of the oddest groups of plant-eating mammals were the chalicotheres. Although they look like a strange mixture of a horse, a bear, and a gorilla, they are close relatives of *Brontotherium*, and more distant relatives of modern horses and rhinos. *Chalicotherium* had long arms, and is equipped with large claws that curved in when it walked. The claws were probably used to scratch up edible roots, or pull together branches to stuff them in the mouth. The skull is horselike, being long and having the jaws lined with deeply-rooted cheek teeth that were used for grinding up plant material. The chalicotheres lived in wooded areas in North America, parts of Europe and Asia, and Africa, where they survived until relatively recently.

Chalicotherium

CHAMPSOSAURUS

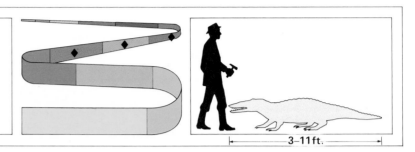

> KAMP-soh-SAW-rus
? Crocodile reptile
ⓝ E. D. Cope (1877)
ⓛ Alberta France
◆ Cretaceous Eocene

3–11 ft.

The champsosaurs look just like crocodiles at first sight. They lived in the lakes and rivers of the midwestern parts of North America, and parts of Europe, during the last few million years of the age of the dinosaurs and the start of the age of mammals. However, *Champsosaurus* was not an early crocodile. In detail, its skull and skeleton seem much more primitive, and seem to share features of the Permian ancestors of the dinosaurs, crocodiles, and lizards. It was clearly a good swimmer since its tail was long and deep, which allowed it to drive the body forward underwater by powerful sideways sweeps. The hands and feet are broad and paddlelike, and they may have been used in swimming or in steering. The long narrow snout, lined with sharp teeth, is the same as that in fish-eating crocodiles. They were obviously highly successful for a time, since they are often the commonest animals found in certain dinosaur deposits.

Champsosaurus

CLAUDIOSAURUS

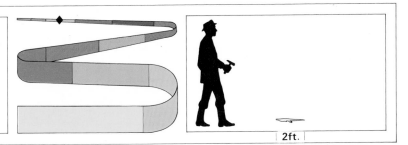

> CLAWD-ee-oh-SAW-rus
? Claude's reptile
ⓝ R. L. Carroll (1981)
ⓛ Madagascar
◆ Permian

2ft.

Skeleton of *Claudiosaurus* (2 feet long)

One of the strangest small reptiles to be found recently has been *Claudiosaurus*. It has a skull that is like that of *Youngina* and a large eye socket and short sharp teeth that were probably used for feeding on insects and small fish. *Claudiosaurus* was clearly a swimming animal since it has broad paddlelike feet that may have been used for "kicking" its way through the water rather like a frog. The tail was also very long, and it might have been used in swimming. *Claudiosaurus* had a relatively small head compared to its body size, and the neck is long.

Claudiosaurus looked rather like a nothosaur or a plesiosaur such as *Cryptocleidus* or *Plesiosaurus*, and it has been suggested that it might be their ancestor. Some details of the skull and skeleton seem to support this idea. The layout of skull openings behind the eye socket is similar, as are some features of the roof of the mouth. The shoulder girdle and the hip girdle also show some similarities to *Nothosaurus* or *Plesiosaurus*. Other scientists have argued that all of these features are also found in other kinds of reptiles as well as the nothosaurs and plesiosaurs. In fact, all swimming reptiles are similar in some respects, and it may be mere coincidence that *Claudiosaurus* looks slightly like a plesiosaur.

43

CLEVOSAURUS

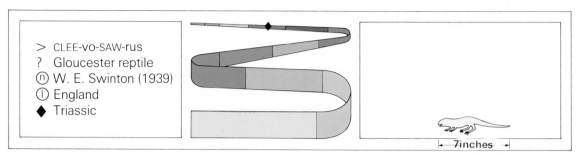

> CLEE-vo-SAW-rus
? Gloucester reptile
ⓝ W. E. Swinton (1939)
① England
◆ Triassic

7inches

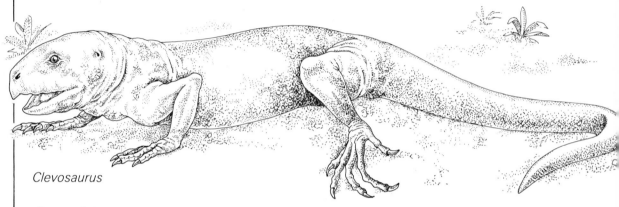

Clevosaurus

One of the most intriguing modern reptiles is the tuatara *Sphenodon* which lives on a few small islands lying off New Zealand. It feeds on insects and worms, hunts partly at night, and can live for a very long time. Indeed tuataras are about 20 years old before they lay eggs, much older than any other reptile. The tuatara looks rather like a lizard, but in detail its skull and skeleton are just like those of the ancestors of modern lizards which lived over 220 million years ago. It is called a "living fossil" because little change seems to have taken place during the evolution of the tuatara line, even during the vast amount of time over which the dinosaurs evolved, died out, and gave rise to the modern mammals.

Clevosaurus is almost identical in every respect to the living tuatara; it differs only in minor features of the teeth and layout of the skull bones. *Clevosaurus* was smaller than the living tuatara, and it may have fed on plants as well as insects, since its teeth were rather different from those of the modern form. *Clevosaurus* is known from many well-preserved bones found in fossilized cave systems in southern England and Wales. The reptiles were presumably walking around above and fell down into the caverns, where they died and were covered over by mud and sand. These famous caves have also produced some of the earliest mammals such as *Morganucodon* as well as other species of tuatara and some dinosaurs.

CRASSIGYRINUS

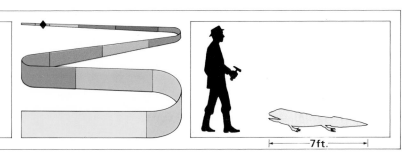

> CRASS-i-ji-RINE-us
? Thick frog
ⓝ D. M. S. Watson (1929)
ⓛ Scotland
◆ Carboniferous

◆ ⟵ 7ft. ⟶

The early history of the amphibians is poorly known. Although *Ichthyostega* is known from rocks dated about 370 million years old, there is a long gap between 360 and 320 million years ago about which little was known until recently. *Crassigyrinus* has a heavy skull with a deep lower jaw. In fact, the lower jaw is as deep as the skull itself. The massive head, and rows of sharp teeth around the jaws, suggest that *Crassigyrinus* may have fed by lunging at fish in shallow ponds. When it opened its huge mouth suddenly, there would have been a huge sucking effect, and muddy water and fish alike would have been sucked in. The whole body of *Crassigyrinus* is now known from some remarkable collections made in Scotland in 1985. It has a long sausagelike body, a deep fishlike tail which was used for swimming, and tiny arms and legs that would have been of little use for walking on land, or much else for that matter!

Crassigyrinus

CRYPTOCLEIDUS

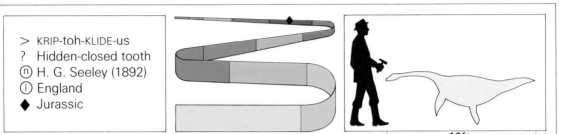

> KRIP-toh-KLIDE-us
? Hidden-closed tooth
ⓝ H. G. Seeley (1892)
ⓛ England
◆ Jurassic

10ft.

Cryptocleidus

The plesiosaurs were important fish-eating reptiles in the seas during the Jurassic and Cretaceous periods. *Cryptocleidus* is a well-known form from England which has a long neck containing about 35 vertebrae, compared to the usual seven or eight in a reptile. The skull and lower jaw are deep, which suggests that there were powerful jaw muscles. *Cryptocleidus* had long and broad paddlehands and feet, both of which were used in swimming. The arms beat up and down in a sort of flying pattern which drew the body forward through the water, and the legs were probably used for steering.

CYNOGNATHUS

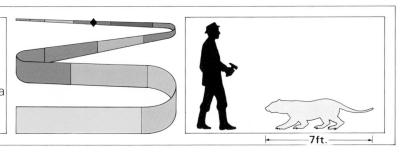

> SY-noh-NAY-thus
? Dog jaw
(n) H. G. Seeley (1896)
(l) Argentina South Africa
♦ Triassic

7 ft.

The mammallike reptiles of the Triassic period (245 to 208 million years ago) became remarkably close to the mammals in many ways. *Cynognathus* probably even had hair. How can we tell that from the fossil bones? Modern mammals often have whiskers on the snout, the long sensitive hairs on either side of the face in cats and dogs for example, which are used to feel objects and even movements in the air round about. Each whisker has a small blood vessel and nerve at the root, and these pass through special openings in the bones of the snout. These openings are found in the skull of *Cynognathus*. If it had whiskers, it must have had

hair covering its body, since whiskers are just a special kind of hair. rather like a large dog such as a German shepherd or a labrador. It had similar teeth: pointed fangs on either side, and sharp triangular-shaped teeth in the cheek region, which show that it was an active hunting meat-eater. *Cynognathus* was an agile runner, but not quite as fast as a modern dog since its legs were shorter and its feet were planted flat on the ground (modern dogs stand up on their toes). The skeleton of *Cynognathus* was mammallike in having a flexible body and a short tail (reptiles usually have long tails).

Cynognathus

DEINOGALERIX

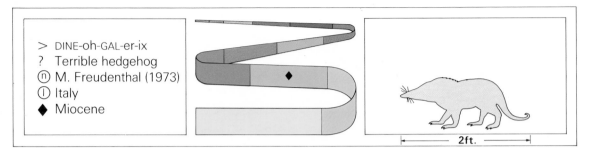

> DINE-oh-GAL-er-ix
? Terrible hedgehog
ⓝ M. Freudenthal (1973)
ⓘ Italy
◆ Miocene

2ft.

One of the most unusual insect-eating mammals was *Deinogalerix*, which was found among cave deposits in southern Italy. This is the largest known hedgehog, three or four times as big as the largest modern form. Indeed, its head alone was longer than the common European hedgehog.

Deinogalerix was a hairy hedgehog, rather than a spiny hedgehog, which means that its body was covered with rough long hair rather than sharp spines. Its 8-inch-long jaws were lined with sharp teeth, and it was so large that it probably ate small lizards and mammals rather than insects and worms, as do modern hedgehogs. Why was *Deinogalerix* so large? It seems that southern Italy at the time was a series of small islands, and *Deinogalerix* probably evolved separately for some time. It might have come to take on the role of a cat or dog since those sorts of meat-eaters were not present on the island.

Deinogalerix

DEINOTHERIUM

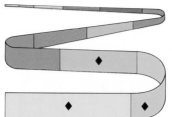

> DINE-oh-THEE-ree-um
? Terrible mammal
ⓝ J. J. Kaup (1829)
ⓛ Europe Asia Africa
◆ Miocene Pliocene
　Pleistocene

13ft.

Today there are only two species of elephants, living in Africa and India, but in the past there were many more. One line of elephant evolution that arose over 40 million years ago and continued until quite recently were the deinotheres, whose fossils were found in Africa, Europe, and Asia. It is clear that *Deinotherium* is some sort of elephant because of the long flexible trunk, the tusks, and the large body size. It was up to 13 feet tall at the shoulder, taller than either of the living elephants.

In detail, the deinotheres clearly became elephantlike separately from the main line of elephant evolution. For example, the tusks are on the lower jaw rather than the upper jaw, as in other true elephants. In addition, the cheek teeth were different in structure, adapted for crushing plant food at the front, and for cutting it up at the back. The cheek teeth of true elephants are used mostly for grinding plant food. The tusks of *Deinotherium* are often heavily worn or broken, and it is likely that they were used for scraping the bark off trees.

Deinotherium

DELTATHERIDIUM

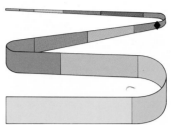
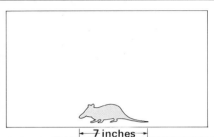

← 7 inches →

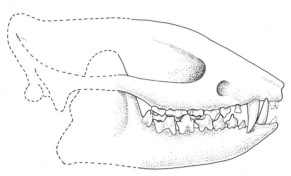

Deltatheridium skull

One of the most intriguing events in the evolution of the mammals was the great split between the pouched marsupials and the placentals which took place some 100 million years ago. These two groups now dominate the world, the marsupials in Australia, and in South America to some extent, and the placentals elsewhere (*see p.90*). The oldest marsupial remains date from about 90 million years ago, while the oldest placentals come from rocks dating from about 85 million years ago. A number of other kinds of mammals were around at the time, and some of these seem to lie about midway between the marsupials and the placentals. *Deltatheridium* is an example of this. It is known from several partial skulls and jaws from the Late Cretaceous of Mongolia. These show some features of placentals and of marsupials in the arrangement of the teeth and the roof of the mouth.

The problems of distinguishing between fossil marsupial and placental mammals are because these two groups have very different ways of producing their young. Marsupials give birth to tiny young which then develop fully inside a pouch. All of these features are "soft" parts which cannot be fossilized. However, there are two tiny bones beneath the pouch of marsupials which help to support it. If these are present in a fossil skeleton, then it clearly is not a placental mammal, and could be a marsupial or a more primitive form. These pouch bones are known in *Ptilodus*, for example. The skeletons of *Deltatheridium* are far too incomplete to tell whether it had the pouch bones or not.

Deltatheridium was larger than most other mammals of its day, being about the size of a rabbit rather than a mouse or rat. It probably fed on insects and small animals.

DIACODEXIS

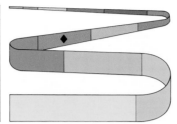

> dy-AK-oh-DEX-is
? Through bite
ⓝ E. D. Cope (1881)
ⓛ North America Europe
◆ Eocene

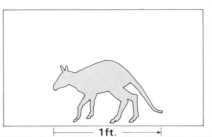

1ft.

One of the most important mammal groups today are the "even-toed" plant-eaters, forms such as cattle, deer, antelope, camels, and pigs. The group has had a long history, but only rose to prominence in the last 10 million years or so. They are called "even-toed" since they have either two or four toes on their feet, rather than one, three, or five. The oldest example is *Diacodexis* from 50-million-year-old rocks in Pakistan. It is a slender lightly-built animal which probably looked more like a rabbit than a cow. However, it has four toes on its feet, a cowlike ankle structure, and teeth which were adapted for crushing leaves.

DIADECTES

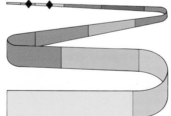

> dy-a-DEK-tees
? Through biter
ⓝ E. D. Cope
ⓛ W. Virginia Ohio Texas
   Pennsylvania
◆ Carboniferous
   Permian

10ft.

The borderline between amphibians and reptiles has been hard to draw, but the vegetarian *Diadectes* appears to lie close to it. This heavily built animal has deep jaws lined with blunt peglike teeth. It had heavy sprawling limbs, and probably could not have moved very fast.

Diadectes

51

DIADEMODON

> DY-a-DEM-o-don
? Crown tooth
Ⓝ H. G. Seeley (1896)
Ⓛ South Africa
◆ Triassic

— 5ft. —

Diademodon represents an unusual side branch of the evolution of the mammallike reptiles. It was a close relative of *Cynognathus*, which lay near to direct descendants of the mammals. However, *Diademodon* and its relatives became highly specialized for coping with very tough plants.

The skull is like that of the meat-eating *Cynognathus*, but the cheek teeth are broad and hard-wearing. Fossil specimens of young examples of *Diademodon* have shown how its teeth were modified. At first, the teeth had a number of small bumps around the edges, just as our cheek teeth do, but these were soon worn away by the tough plant food, leaving a cylinder of hard enamel surrounding a core of the softer dentine in the middle. The remarkable feature of these teeth was that those in the upper jaw worked precisely against those in the lower. This is the case with our teeth, and those of other mammals, but it is not at all typical of reptiles.

The snout in *Diademodon* is narrow, but the skull becomes broad at the back. The great square spaces

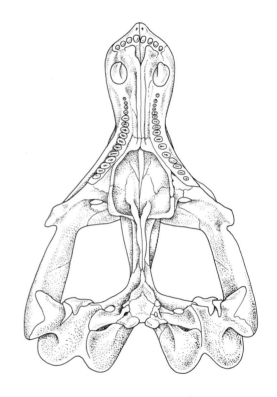

Diademodon skull

on either side at the back were filled with jaw muscles, so that *Diademodon* must have had a powerful bite, and it could have ground up the toughest stems and leaves. In some ways, *Diademodon* may be seen as the first in a long line of successful animals, a kind of reptilian rat, although it is not specifically related to the rodents.

DIATRYMA

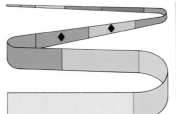

> DY-a-TRY-ma
? Through hole
ⓝ W. D. Matthew and
   W. Granger
Ⓛ Europe North America
◆ Paleocene Eocene

7ft.

Diatryma

In the early years of the age of the mammals, after the dinosaurs had all disappeared, some very strange animals emerged. For a time, about 65 to 40 million years ago, the largest meat-eaters in parts of Europe and North America were flightless birds. *Diatryma* reached about human size and had a large head with massive jaws. It hunted all of the small and medium-sized mammals of its day and could quite easily have captured an early horse such as *Hyracotherium*, which lived at the same time.

DICYNODON

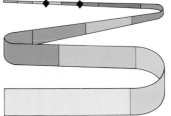
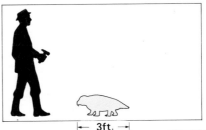

> dy-SY-no-don
? Two dog teeth
ⓝ R. Owen (1845)
Ⓛ South Africa
◆ Permian Triassic

— 3ft. —

When the mammallike reptiles ruled the Earth, before the dinosaurs came to prominence, the main plant-eaters were the dicynodonts, a group of small to large pig-shaped animals. *Dicynodon* had lost most of its teeth, and it cut up plant food with its sharp horn-covered jaws.

DIDUS

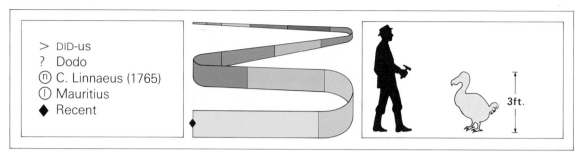

> DID-us
? Dodo
ⓝ C. Linnaeus (1765)
ⓘ Mauritius
◆ Recent

3ft.

The dodo, *Didus ineptus*, is probably the most famous animal to have been killed off by humans. This strange heavily built land bird was discovered by Dutch sailors on the island of Mauritius in 1598. Two specimens were brought back to Europe, where they were exhibited to the wonderment of all. They were described in the account of this voyage in a book published in 1601 which noted that "we called these birds disgusting birds for the reason that the more and the longer they were cooked, the less soft and more unpalatable their flesh becomes."

Unfortunately, other sailors found the dodo was quite a tasty bird. It was so large and heavy, that a single bird could feed half the crew of a typical merchant ship for a day. The name dodo is based on the Portuguese word "*doudo*" which means "simpleton," and the seamen chose that name because the birds were so easy to catch.

The dodo was covered with gray feathers, except over its face which had bare skin. It was flightless, and had small stumpy wings and a strange tuft of feathers for a tail. Its massive curved beak was used for cracking seeds. It had existed for thousands of years with no competition. This explains why dodos were so tame that the seamen could capture them easily. Unfortunately, the ships also brought rats and dogs which escaped onto the islands and ate dodo eggs. The last living dodo was seen in 1681 by an English visitor; it had taken less than 100 years to kill off all examples of this remarkable bird.

Dimetrodon

DIMETRODON

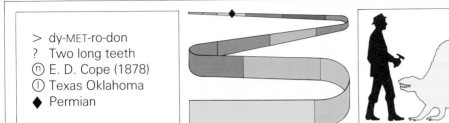

> dy-MET-ro-don
? Two long teeth
ⓝ E. D. Cope (1878)
Ⓛ Texas Oklahoma
◆ Permian

10ft.

The sail-backed reptiles of Early Permian times, some 280 to 260 million years ago, are well-known mammallike reptiles. *Dimetrodon* had a large head, with broadly curved, almost "smiling," jaws lined with sharp teeth, and it presumably fed on other smaller sail-backs, as well as animals like *Captorhinus* and *Eryops* which lived at the same time. *Dimetrodon* had primitive limbs that sprawl out to the side, but they were more slender than in many forms of the time, so it was probably slightly more agile than its prey. The most striking feature was the large sail on its back.

DIMORPHODON

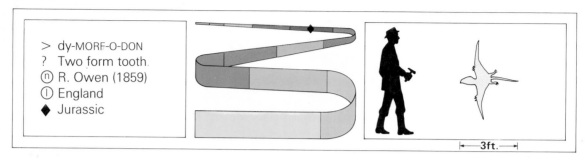

> dy-MORF-O-DON
? Two form tooth.
Ⓝ R. Owen (1859)
Ⓛ England
◆ Jurassic

—3ft.—

For a long time *Dimorphodon* was the oldest known pterosaur, or flying reptile. Several partial skeletons had been found over the past 150 years on the south coast of England in rocks laid down under the sea. The other fossils included ichthyosaurs, plesiosaurs, and marine shells, and it was assumed that *Dimorphodon* had flown out over the shallow sea to catch fish when it drowned and fell to the bottom. Older pterosaurs are now known from the Late Triassic, some 15 million years earlier.

Nevertheless, *Dimorphodon* is an important animal. Its skeleton is quite well known, and shows it to have been rather unusual. The head was huge, being bigger than the body, and the purpose of the heavy jaws is uncertain. The neck is long, the rib cage very small, as in all pterosaurs, and the tail is long. The tail was stiffened in life by long bony rods that ran down each side. It has been suggested recently that *Dimorphodon* ran about on land like a small dinosaur, and that it used its long stiff tail as a kind of balancing rod. The wing is supported mainly by a long finger and the wing was made from skin, as in modern bats. It is likely that *Dimorphodon* lived rather like a seagull, feeding on fish over the shallow seas.

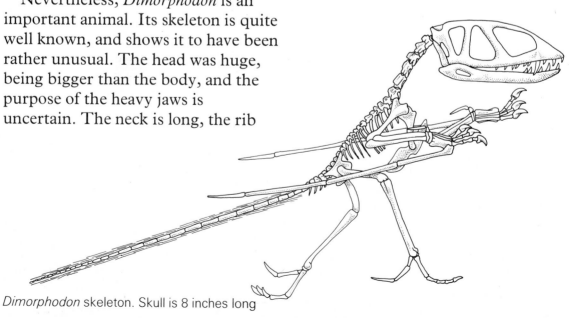

Dimorphodon skeleton. Skull is 8 inches long

DINILYSIA

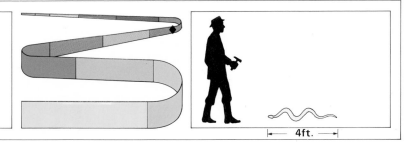

> DY-nil-i-see-a
? Terrible destroyer
Ⓝ A. S. Woodward (1901)
Ⓛ South Africa
◆ Cretaceous

The snakes arose from lizard ancestors about 130 million years ago. The oldest reasonably known snake specimen is *Dinilysia*. It was a non-poisonous snake that killed by suffocating its prey in tightening coils, like the modern-day pythons and boa constrictors. It could then swallow whole, quite large animals by loosening the jaw bones.

Dinilysia skull (4 inches long)

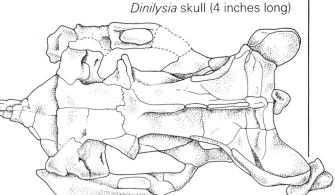

DINOCERAS

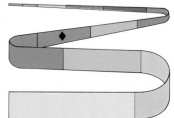 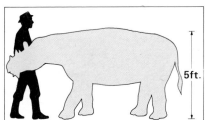

> dy-NO-ser-as
? Terrible horn
Ⓝ O. C. Marsh (1871)
Ⓛ Utah Mongolia
◆ Eocene

5ft.

The uintatheres were large plant-eaters that lived in the first 30 million years of the age of the mammals in North America and central Asia. *Dinoceras*, a typical uintathere, was as large as a rhinoceros, but in no way related to this modern form. Its skull was adorned by three pairs of bony knobs, two above the nostrils, two above the eyes, and two at the back. In addition, the males had a pair of long knifelike fangs. These terrifying knobs and fangs were probably used in fighting between males or for defense, although there were few meat-eaters around at the time that could have tackled *Dinoceras*.

DIPLOCAULUS

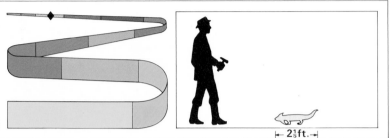

> di-plo-KAWL-us
? Two fold stem
Ⓝ E. D. Cope (1877)
Ⓛ Texas
◆ Permian

← 2½ ft. →

Diplocaulus

Some early amphibians became specialized as salamanderlike forms, although they are in no way related to modern salamanders. One of these "salamanderlike" lines of the Carboniferous gave rise to the peculiar *Diplocaulus* in the Early Permian, some 270 million years ago. The body is rather like a standard newt or salamander, but its head has a remarkable pair of bony "horns" that stick out sideways, giving the head the overall shape of a boomerang.

This moderately-sized animal was common in its day and dozens of skeletons have been collected, from newly hatched babies to fully grown adults with their 9-inch wide skulls.

These show that the "horns" were not really horns at all, but simply outgrowths of the bones that normally make up the cheek region of the skull. As the animal grew up, two or three of the skull bones in the back corner just grew out and out until the triangular wing was formed. What was it for? One idea is that it was a kind of wing used in underwater swimming to keep the head up. Another idea is that the "horns" helped *Diplocaulus* to open its mouth rapidly and swim up from the bottom of a pond quickly, underneath an unsuspecting fish. It may simply be that the "horns" were for protection, to stop larger animals from trying to swallow *Diplocaulus*.

DIPROTODON

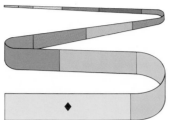

> dy-PROTE-o-don
? Two first teeth
(n) R. Owen (1870)
(l) Australia
◆ Pleistocene

10ft.

One of the most remarkable Australian marsupial mammals was the giant wombat *Diprotodon*. The diprotodonts arose some 12 million years ago, and lived right through to a few thousand years ago. *Diprotodon* was a rhinoceros-sized monster plant-eater that ranged in large herds across southern and central parts of Australia. *Diprotodon* had a large head with long front teeth for cropping leaves from low bushes, and broad flat cheek teeth behind for grinding them up. The legs were massively built, to support the animal's great weight, and the feet were broad and equipped with claws. *Diprotodon* is equivalent in many ways to the rhinoceroses elsewhere in the world, was probably slow-moving, and it may have been hunted to extinction by the first Australian aborigines.

Diprotodon

EDAPHOSAURUS

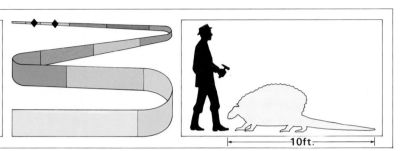

> eh-DAF-o-SAW-rus
? Earth reptile
(n) E. D. Cope (1883)
(l) Oklahoma Texas
  Germany
◆ Carboniferous
  Permian

10ft.

Edaphosaurus was a plant-eating sail-backed reptile, unlike *Dimetrodon* but like *Casea*, another relative which did not have a sail. *Edaphosaurus* had a tiny head with small peglike teeth, a heavy body, small legs, a long tail, and a sail on its back. In life, the sail was covered with skin that carried a rich blood supply that was used to control the reptile's body

temperature. Early in the morning, when the air was cool, they would stand sideways to the sun, and the weak morning rays heated the blood in the sail, which then passed around the body. At midday, when the heat of the sun may have been too great, *Edaphosaurus* could shelter, and use its sail as a radiator to give off heat and cool the body.

Edaphosaurus

ELASMOSAURUS

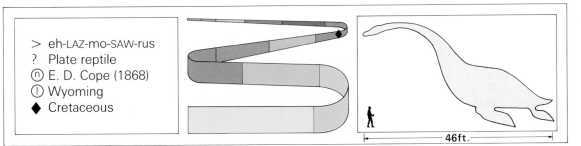

> eh-LAZ-mo-SAW-rus
? Plate reptile
Ⓝ E. D. Cope (1868)
Ⓛ Wyoming
◆ Cretaceous

46ft.

Most of the plesiosaurs, such as
Cryptocleidus and *Plesiosaurus*, had
fairly long necks, but *Elasmosaurus*
and its relatives take the record, with
necks that were longer than the rest of
the body and tail together. There
were as many as 75 vertebrae in the
neck, compared to the usual seven or
eight in most land animals.

    Elasmosaurus had a tiny head, and it
probably swung its neck around
under water almost like a snake, as it
chased fast-moving fish. This may
have been an efficient way to operate
since it meant that *Elasmosaurus* could
hunt fish by moving its head and neck
alone, and not chasing them by
moving its whole body, which would
have been a rather slower operation.
The paddles were very long, and they
were probably used for swimming in
a kind of underwater flying as in
modern penguins and sea turtles.

Elasmosaurus

EOGYRINUS

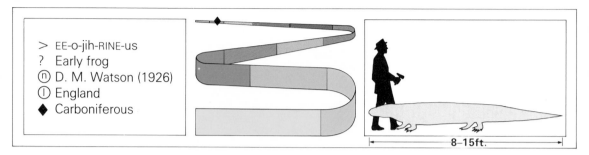

> EE-o-jih-RINE-us
? Early frog
ⓝ D. M. Watson (1926)
Ⓘ England
◆ Carboniferous

8–15ft.

Some of the early amphibians of the Carboniferous became aquatic in their habits. For example, *Eogyrinus* seems to have had such short limbs that it would have been able to move only very slowly on land. It probably could not have lifted its belly from the ground. However, its tail was deep and flattened, an ideal structure for swimming by powerful sideways movements. In the water, the arms and legs may have been used simply for steering. The long body of *Eogyrinus* is an unusual feature; it had nearly twice as many vertebrae in its backbone as in typical amphibians or reptiles.

The first specimens of *Eogyrinus* were found in the coal workings of northern England in the 1870s, and several specimens have been found since then. The skull is well enough known to reconstruct how it operated. It is deeper than the skulls of some of the other lines of amphibians such as *Crassigyrinus* or *Eryops* and this allowed longer jaw muscles. Hence, *Eogyrinus* may have had a stronger bite, like that of a crocodile, than some of its contemporaries. It may have fed on fish in the ponds in the coal swamps, or on other amphibians which it caught near the water's edge.

Eogyrinus

E

EOMANIS

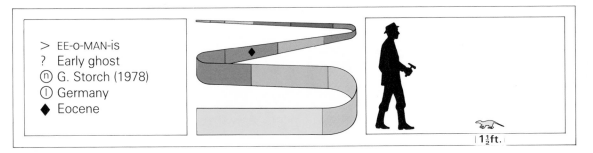

> EE-o-MAN-is
? Early ghost
Ⓝ G. Storch (1978)
Ⓛ Germany
◆ Eocene

1½ft.

Eomanis

The pangolins, or scaly anteaters, are some of the most peculiar, and rarest, modern mammals. There are seven living species, to be found in Africa and Southeast Asia, but their fossil record is rather poor. A remarkable find, made in Germany in 1978, was of the oldest known fossil pangolin, *Eomanis*. This find was unexpected, as modern pangolins live so far from Germany.

Eomanis has a long tubular skull with no teeth at all, and a weak lower jaw that was not much use for anything. Like modern pangolins, *Eomanis* probably had a long muscular tongue which could be used to lick up ants by the dozen. The exact diet of *Eomanis* is known since the remains of its last meal are preserved in the stomach region within the fossil skeleton. These include insect remains as well as plant fragments. *Eomanis* shows the other characteristic features of pangolins. The limbs are short and equipped with long claws which were used to dig into the nests of ants and termites. In addition, the body is covered with broad overlapping scales made from a material like our finger nails. No doubt *Eomanis* could curl up into an armored ball if it was threatened, just as its modern relatives do.

EPIGAULUS

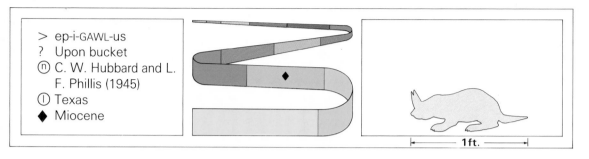

> ep-i-GAWL-us
? Upon bucket
ⓝ C. W. Hubbard and L. F. Phillis (1945)
ⓛ Texas
◆ Miocene

1ft.

The great mammalian group of the rodents has been very successful, and it includes such common living forms as mice, rats, squirrels, beavers, and porcupines. In the past, there were some unusual rodents, of which *Epigaulus* must be the most singular. It probably looked rather like a beaver, but it had a pair of horns on its nose. *Epigaulus* lived in forest areas of the Great Basin region of the midwestern United States, and it dug burrows with the long claws on its hands and feet. Why would a burrowing rodent need horns? It may be that they were used for fighting between males, since some skeletons seem to have horns, while others (possibly females) do not. *Epigaulus* had deep-rooted cheek teeth that were used to grind up tough plant food, but the group died out when the forests in the area were replaced by open grasslands.

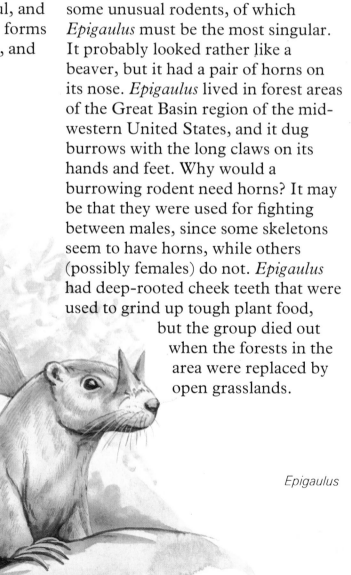

Epigaulus

ERYOPS

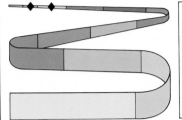

> ER-ee-ops
? Draw face
ⓝ E. D. Cope (1887)
① Oklahoma Texas
◆ Carboniferous
  Permian

7ft.

Some of the amphibians of the Permian became adapted to life on land, while other forms, such as *Eogyrinus* were water-dwellers. One of the land-livers was the well-known *Eryops* which lived side by side with sail-backed reptiles such as *Dimetrodon* and *Edaphosaurus*. It may have fed on smaller amphibians and reptiles, or on fish. *Eryops* had longer legs than many of its more aquatic relatives, but these were still rather clumsy, and it probably could not run fast. *Eryops* also had another primitive feature, its large low head, which had little room for advanced jaw muscles, or for brains for that matter!

Eryops and its relatives from the Early Permian of North America might seem to have been doomed to extinction since they lived side by side with much more agile early reptiles. It is now believed that the modern amphibian groups, the frogs, newts, and salamanders, arose from forms rather like *Eryops*. There may seem to be a long way between *Eryops* and a frog or salamander, but the oldest known frog, *Triadobatrachus*, which lived about 20 million years later shows how one could have evolved into the other. The modern forms still have broad rounded low skulls, large eyes, small pointed teeth, and small sprawling legs. Frogs got their long jumping legs later.

Eryops

ERYTHROSUCHUS

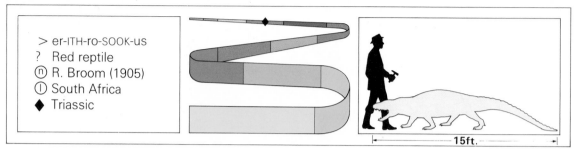

> er-ITH-ro-SOOK-us
? Red reptile
ⓝ R. Broom (1905)
ⓛ South Africa
◆ Triassic

15ft.

The dinosaurs and crocodiles arose from an important group of Triassic reptiles called the thecodontians, and *Erythrosuchus* was one of the earliest forms. It was larger than its relative *Proterosuchus*, and was the largest meat-eater of its day. *Erythrosuchus* had a large skull with strong jaws, and it fed on the plant-eating dicynodonts which were so common then. The erythrosuchids lived almost everywhere in the Early Triassic, but they soon gave way to more advanced relatives such as *Ornithosuchus* and *Ticinosuchus*.

ESTEMMENOSUCHUS

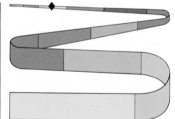
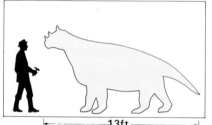

> es-TEM-en-o-SOOK-us
? Strong garment reptile
ⓝ P. K. Chudinov (1913)
ⓛ Russia
◆ Permian

13ft.

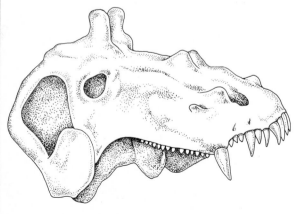

Estemmenosuchus skull (32 inches long)

The mammallike reptiles of the Late Permian were very varied and included *Estemmenosuchus*. This giant Russian form had long sharp front teeth, but tiny cheek teeth behind, which shows that it ate plants. The skull is made from heavy bone, and it bears a number of bony knobs in pairs over the snout and forehead. It may be that male *Estemmenosuchus* used them in fighting for mates.

EUPARKERIA

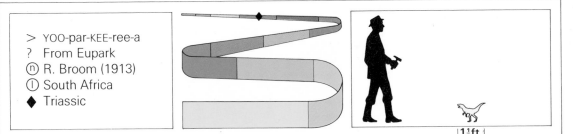

> YOO-par-KEE-ree-a
? From Eupark
ⓝ R. Broom (1913)
Ⓛ South Africa
◆ Triassic

|1½ft.|

Euparkeria

The thecodontians, which include the ancestors of the crocodiles and dinosaurs, led to a number of unusual forms during the Triassics such as *Erythrosuchus*, *Parasuchus*, and *Stagonolepis*. One small animal, *Euparkeria*, seems to be close to the origins of both the crocodilian line and the dinosaurian line. It had a lightly-built skeleton, and was probably able to walk on all fours, or rear up on its hind legs to run fast. It fed on meat, as is clear from its daggerlike teeth, but it could probably only tackle smaller plant-eaters such as small mammallike reptiles or *Procolophon*.

Euparkeria is important since it seems to show ancestral features of the dinosaur line seen also in the later *Ornithosuchus*. This is not absolutely certain, and *Euparkeria* may lie at the base of both the crocodilians and dinosaurs, before the two groups evolved along their separate ways. Scientists still cannot decide on this question since the evolutionary changes are seen best in the ankle structure, and those of *Euparkeria* are badly preserved.

GEOSAURUS

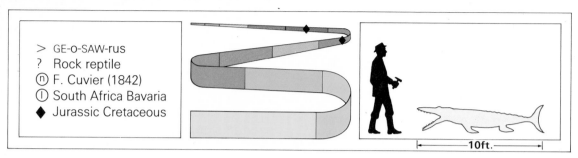

> GE-o-SAW-rus
? Rock reptile
Ⓝ F. Cuvier (1842)
Ⓛ South Africa Bavaria
◆ Jurassic Cretaceous

10ft.

Crocodilians today generally live both in water and on the land. Some fossil forms, such as *Geosaurus*, were highly modified to live in the water nearly all of the time. The hands and feet were broad and paddlelike, while the tail was bent downward near the end and bore a fleshy tail fin in life, just as in the unrelated *Ichthyosaurus*. The neck was short and the head relatively big, as in some other swimming meat-eaters like *Pliosaurus*. The sharp teeth show that *Geosaurus* fed on fish. In addition, it had no bony armor plates over the body, as in typical crocodilians, and this may have made it more streamlined. The skeletons of *Geosaurus* have been found in sediments laid down in the seas of central Europe.

Geosaurus

GERROTHORAX

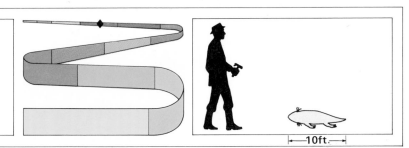

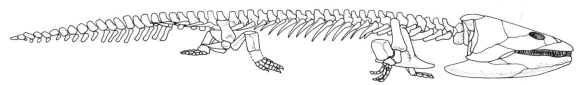

Gerrothorax skeleton and (*below*) skull

The primitive amphibians which dominated the Earth during the Carboniferous lived on for many millions of years after the reptiles and modern amphibians (frogs and salamanders) had emerged. One group that lived on were the plagiosaurs such as *Gerrothorax*, which are known best from the Triassic, 50 million years or more after the Carboniferous. The last plagiosaurs may have disappeared finally in the Cretaceous, another 120 million years later. The only evidence is a partial skull from Australia that was only recognized as being a plagiosaur quite recently.

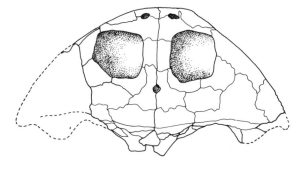

Gerrothorax was a bulky animal with an extremely short wide skull that is covered with rough patterns of sculpture on the bone. Some relatives seem to have gills even as adults. These may be like the "adult tadpoles" seen today among many salamander groups, and also in the fossil *Branchiosaurus*. This may partly explain the odd shape of *Gerrothorax*, the idea is that it is a giant tadpole that never transformed into a different adult form. Hence, *Gerrothorax* and its relatives may have lived a life fully in the water, feeding on fish. In this way, they may have found themselves a mode of life that none of the mammallike reptiles or dinosaurs was able to copy, and hence they were able to survive long after their relatives had died out.

GLYPTODON

> GLIP-toh-don
? Carved tooth
ⓝ R. Owen (1839)
① Argentina Brazil
◆ Pleistocene

The armadillos of the Americas today are rabbit-sized animals covered with an armor of flexible bands that feed on ants and termites. The group seems to have lived in South America for 60 million years or so, and shows little change. A remarkable side branch, the glyptodonts, arose some 45 million years ago. One of the later members, *Glyptodon*, was as large as a rhinoceros, and covered with a vast carapace of armor to protect it from the sabre-toothed "cats" of South America, such as *Thylacosmilus*. The armor was made from irregular circular plates of bone that fitted together closely like a mosaic. There was also a patch of armor on top of the head, and the tail was covered with overlapping spiny rings of bone. It is likely that *Glyptodon* did not feed on ants, like its modern relatives, but upon grass and other tough plants. This remarkable form died out only a few thousand years ago, at the same time as *Megatherium*.

Glyptodon

GOMPHOTHERIUM

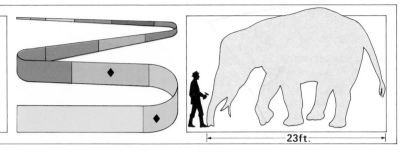

> GOM-foh-THEE-ree-um
? Nail beast
ⓝ F. Cuvier (1806)
ⓛ Europe Africa North America Asia
◆ Miocene Pliocene

23ft.

The Miocene, some 25 to 5 million years ago, was in many ways the age of elephants. There were dozens of species of elephants in all parts of the world, rather than just the present two species. *Gomphotherium* is distinguished by having a pair of tusks in both the upper jaw and the lower jaw: four tusks in all. The lower tusks are broad and shovellike and these may have been used to plow up plant roots or water plants for food.

Gomphotherium lived in many parts of the world, from Kenya to Pakistan and France to North America, and several species are known. It is uncertain why elephants have declined so much since the Miocene, but it may have something to do with the fact that some parts of the world in which the gomphotheres lived are now too cold or too full of people.

GREERERPETON

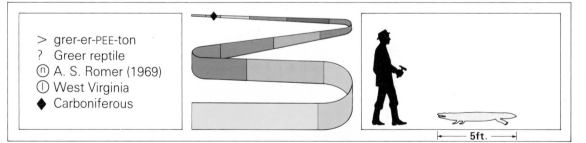

> grer-er-PEE-ton
? Greer reptile
ⓝ A. S. Romer (1969)
ⓛ West Virginia
◆ Carboniferous

5ft.

Major events took place in the evolution of amphibians during the Early Carboniferous, with the split into one amphibian line that led to modern frogs and salamanders, and another line that led to the reptiles.

Greererpeton, a rare form from West Virginia, seems to be an early form on the amphibian side. It was an aquatic form, with a long body, short limbs, and a heavy head.

GRIPPIA

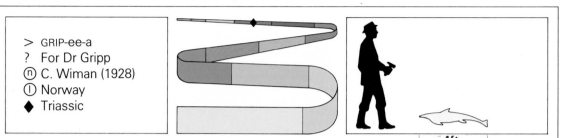

> GRIP-ee-a
? For Dr Gripp
ⓝ C. Wiman (1928)
ⓛ Norway
◆ Triassic

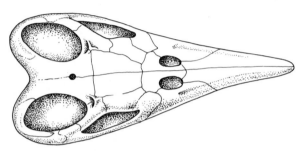

Grippia skull (6 inches long), dorsal (rear) and lateral (side) views

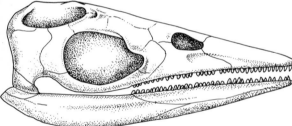

One of the great mysteries of the Mesozoic, the age of the dinosaurs, is the origin of the various groups of marine reptiles, the ichthyosaurs, nothosaurs, plesiosaurs, and placodonts. All four groups seem to have arisen in the Triassic, from 245 to 208 million years ago, as fully developed swimming animals, with all of the special characteristics of their groups. They all arose from land-living forms, but which ones? One important find was *Grippia*, which is the oldest well-preserved ichthyosaur skull. At first sight, it looks like the later typical ichthyosaurs such as *Ichthyosaurus*. The snout and jaws are much shorter than in later ichthyosaurs, and the bones of the skull roof and those behind the large eye sockets are not so closely set.

Grippia shows some special features of its own. For example, the teeth are not all long and sharp, as in later ichthyosaurs. At the back of the jaws, there are two rows of blunt rounded teeth which seem to be more adapted for crushing shellfish, as in *Placodus*, than for piercing fish. The skeleton of *Grippia* is not well known, but other early ichthyosaurs from China and Japan show that its arms and legs were probably halfway between being walking limbs and paddles. They are broader, flatter, and shorter than the arms and legs of land reptiles, but in no way as modified as the paddles of *Ichthyosaurus*. It is still uncertain which land reptiles gave rise to the ichthyosaurs, but *Grippia* and other early forms suggest that they may have arisen from some thecodontian that lived before *Proterosuchus*.

HESPERORNIS

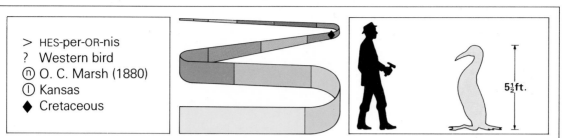

> HES-per-OR-nis
? Western bird
ⓝ O. C. Marsh (1880)
ⓛ Kansas
◆ Cretaceous

5½ft.

The early fossil record of birds is patchy. There is a particularly long gap during the Cretaceous after the extinction of *Archaeopteryx*, lasting for some 60 million years, during which only a few isolated bones and partial skeletons are known. In the Late Cretaceous, some excellent bird skeletons are known from limestones that were laid down in shallow seas in the mid-western region of the United States. These bird remains include *Hesperornis* and *Ichthyornis*. *Hesperornis* was a diving bird that probably looked like a large loon or cormorant. It had large feet that may have been webbed and were used in swimming, while the wings are reduced to small splints of bone that may have been used for steering under water, but which certainly could not have been used for flight.

Hesperornis is intermediate in many ways between *Archaeopteryx* and modern birds. For example, it still has teeth in its beak, and the bony tail is fairly long.

Hesperornis

73

EVOLUTION OF THE HUMANS

Humans belong to the Order Primates, a group of mammals that also includes monkeys and apes. The oldest known primate, *Purgatorius*, probably looked more like a squirrel or a rat than a monkey. That it was a primate is shown by the teeth, and it probably had strong grasping hands and a large brain. Other early primates, like *Plesiadapis* and *Smilodectes*, were approximately cat-sized and like living lemurs. They had long tails, good eyesight, and ran about in the trees with great agility.

The first true monkeys arose some 40 million years ago, and they split into two groups, the New World monkeys in South America, and the Old World monkeys in Africa, Asia, and Europe. The two groups can be told apart because New World monkeys have broad noses with nostrils facing forward and their tails can grasp branches like a fifth leg. The Old World monkeys have narrow noses and non-grasping tails.

The apes arose from Old World monkeys about 30 million years ago, and were important in Africa and other parts of the world, with early ground-living forms like *Proconsul* and *Ramapithecus*. Apes today include the gibbons, orangs, gorillas, and chimps, as well as humans.

The oldest humans arose about 5 million years ago, and the first fossils include the famous footprints in ash from 3.75 million years ago (*see page 14*), as well as skeletons of *Australopithecus* from rocks dating from 1–3.5 million years ago. *Australopithecus* is known to be the

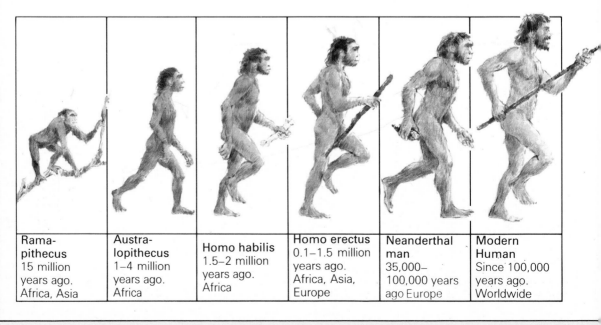

Rama-pithecus 15 million years ago. Africa, Asia	Austra-lopithecus 1–4 million years ago. Africa	Homo habilis 1.5–2 million years ago. Africa	Homo erectus 0.1–1.5 million years ago. Africa, Asia, Europe	Neanderthal man 35,000– 100,000 years ago Europe	Modern Human Since 100,000 years ago. Worldwide

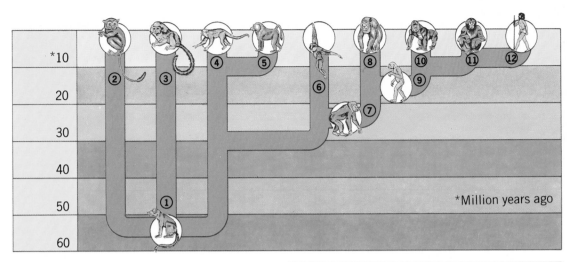

first human, because it could stand and walk fully upright, as we do.

Modern humans belong to the species *Homo sapiens*, which means "wise person." Some earlier human species which were very like us include *Homo habilis* and *Homo erectus*. Unlike *Australopithecus*, these two had large brains, as we do, and they could make tools and fire. *Homo sapiens* arose about 100,000 years ago. A human subspecies, Neanderthal man, lived for some time after this in the cold ice ages of Europe, but died

out 35,000 years ago. All modern humans are closely related, and stemmed from the 100,000 year old ancestor in Africa.

20,000 years ago, humans lived in caves and used stone tools to kill animals to eat.

Key to human evolution	
1 Plesiadapsis	7 Dryopithecus
2 Tarsier	8 Orangutan
3 Marmoset	9 Ramapithecus
4 Diana monkey	10 Gorilla
5 Baboon	11 Chimpanzee
6 Gibbon	12 Human being

HOVASAURUS

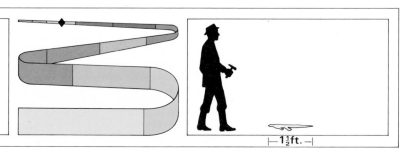

> HOVE-a-SAW-rus
? Hova reptile
Ⓝ J. Piveteau (1926)
Ⓛ Madagascar
◆ Permian

> 1½ft.

The Late Permian deposits of Madagascar have produced many remarkable small reptiles, including the gliding *Weigeltisaurus* and the swimming *Hovasaurus*. *Hovasaurus* had a remarkably long deep tail that beat from side to side to drive the

Hovasaurus skeleton (20 inches long)

animal through the water. It seems to be closely related to the land-living *Youngina*, and belongs to a group that is related to the ancestors of the lizards.

HYAENODON

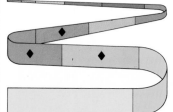
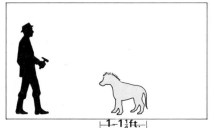

> hy-EE-no-don
? Hyena tooth
Ⓝ M. de Laizer and L. de Parieu (1838)
Ⓛ Europe Asia Africa North America
◆ Eocene Miocene

> 1–1¼ft.

During the first half of the age of mammals, the main meat-eaters outside South America and Australia were not the modern carnivores, such as cats, dogs, and bears, but an earlier broad group, the creodonts, such as *Hyaenodon* and *Oxyaena*. *Hyaenodon* includes species as small as a stoat,

and others as large as a hyena. The head is relatively large, and the jaws are lined with sharp teeth, as in modern cats and dogs. The legs were long and slender, and *Hyaenodon* was evidently a fast runner which could have hunted most of the plant-eaters of its day.

HYLONOMUS

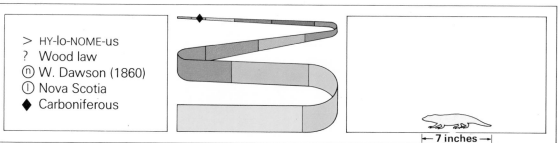

> HY-lo-NOME-us
? Wood law
ⓝ W. Dawson (1860)
Ⓛ Nova Scotia
◆ Carboniferous

← 7 inches →

Hylonomous

Until recently, *Hylonomus* was generally regarded as the oldest known reptile. The skeletons of *Hylonomus* were found in fossilized tree stumps, just like those of *Archaeothyris*. The hollow tree stumps acted as traps for these early reptiles, which fell into them, but they also allowed their small skeletons to be well preserved to the present day. *Hylonomus* probably looked like a moderate-sized lizard, although it was more heavily built, and was not closely related to the modern lizards. The solid little skull bore rows of sharp teeth around the margins of the jaws which suggests that *Hylonomus* fed on the large insects and centipedes of the coal-forest floor. There were also teeth in the roof of the mouth, a primitive feature, and these probably worked against horny "teeth" on the tongue to break up the food. *Hylonomus* may no longer be the oldest reptile after a discovery made in 1988 in Scotland. A skeleton of a reptile has been reported from rocks dating from 40 million years before *Hylonomus*, but it is not so well preserved.

HYOPSODUS

> HY-op-SOE-dus
? Hog tooth
ⓝ J. Leidy (1870)
ⓛ North America Asia
◆ Paleocene Eocene

← 7 inches →

In the early years of the age of the mammals, over 45 million years ago, the main plant-eating mammals in North America and Europe were condylarths such as *Hyopsodus* and *Phenacodus*. *Hyopsodus* was slightly larger than a hedgehog. Its teeth were not so specialized for plant-eating as in modern forms, but the cheek teeth were broad and flat which shows that they were used for grinding up leaves. *Hyopsodus* had short limbs and may have been able to climb trees. This animal was once thought to be ancestral to the "even-toed" plant-eaters, such as the pigs, cattle, deer, and camels, but there is no special evidence for this suggestion.

HYPERODAPEDON

> HY-per-o-DAP-e-don
? Upper pavement tooth
ⓝ T. H. Huxley (1859)
ⓛ India Scotland
◆ Triassic

← 4ft. →

Just before the dinosaurs came on the scene, rhynchosaurs such as *Hyperodapedon* were the predominant plant-eaters. These unusual reptiles had pig-sized bodies and heavy skulls. Their jaws bear many rows of teeth and the lower jaw closed firmly into a groove in the upper jaw, rather like the blade of a penknife closing into its handle.

Hyperodapedon skeleton (5 feet long)

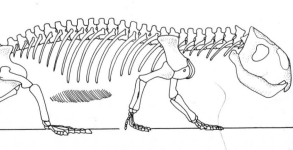

HYRACOTHERIUM

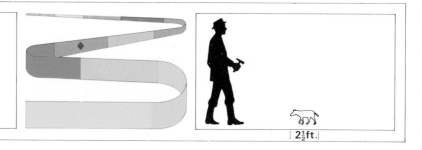

?	Mole beast
n	R. Owen (1841)
l	England Wyoming Asia
◆	Eocene

2½ ft.

Hyracotherium

The story of the evolution of horses is well known. The first horse was *Hyracotherium*, a small terrier-sized animal, that probably did not look much like a horse. It had short legs with four toes on its feet and a dog-like skull with low teeth. It probably lived a secretive life in the undergrowth of the thick subtropical forests that covered North America and Europe 50 million years ago, feeding on leaves and shoots.

The first fossils of *Hyracotherium* were found in England about 140 years ago. Later, some early horse remains were found in North America and named *Eohippus*, or "dawn horse." Later, it became clear that *Eohippus* was the same as the European *Hyracotherium*. At the same time, a series of fossil horses was found that seemed to link the tiny forest-living *Hyracotherium* with the modern large grassland horse.

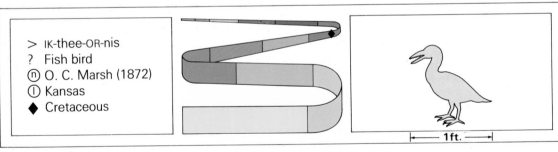

ICARONYCTERIS

> IK-ar-o-NICT-er-us
? Icarus bat
ⓝ Russel, Louis and Savage (1973)
ⓛ France
◆ Eocene

4 inches

Bats are like flying shrews or mice. They are mammals because they have hair and they feed their young with milk, and yet they fly as well as birds, though they hunt insects at night and sleep by day. The bats arose from some normal land-living mammal, but their origin is still a mystery. The oldest known bat, *Icaronycteris*, gives few clues since it is a fully developed bat, with a lightweight skeleton and large wings made from skin stretched over its long narrow finger bones. It even shows evidence that the ears were able to pick up the high-pitched squeaks that modern bats make to find their way around in the dark.

ICHTHYORNIS

> IK-thee-OR-nis
? Fish bird
ⓝ O. C. Marsh (1872)
ⓛ Kansas
◆ Cretaceous

1 ft.

Ichthyornis

The marine limestones in North America that contain fossils of the large flightless diving bird *Hesperornis* have also produced *Ichthyornis*, a more advanced form. It could fly, and may have looked rather like a seagull. It was still a primitive form since it had teeth in its jaws.

ICHTHYOSAURUS

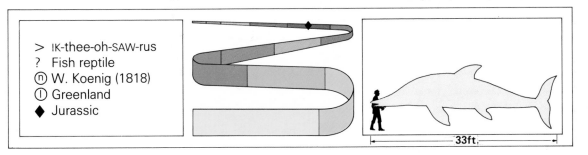

> IK-thee-oh-SAW-rus
? Fish reptile
ⓝ W. Koenig (1818)
ⓛ Greenland
◆ Jurassic

33ft.

The dolphinlike ichthyosaurs were important fish-eaters in the seas of the Jurassic world. They had become more streamlined and faster at swimming than their ancestral form, *Grippia*. Some of the fossils of *Ichthyosaurus* from Germany are so well preserved that details of the skin may be seen as a black outline around the bones. This shows that they had a smooth plump fish-shaped body. The long narrow snout cut through the water, and a narrow sharklike fin on the back helped to make the body move more easily.

Ichthyosaurus swam by beating its high, narrow tail from side to side. This is one of the few obvious differences from modern dolphins, which are mammals: they beat their flat tails up and down to swim. Some of the best preserved skeletons of *Ichthyosaurus* have remains of their last meals inside the rib cage, and these include parts of cuttlefish and other shellfish, as well as fish.

Ichthyosaurus

ICHTHYOSTEGA

> IK-thee-O-STEEG-a
? Fish spine
ⓝ G. Säve-Söderbergh (1932)
Ⓛ England Germany France
◆ Devonian

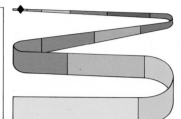

|←——3ft.——→|

Ichthyostega

At present *Ichthyostega* is the oldest and most clearly identified land vertebrate, the ancestor of all the later amphibians, reptiles, birds, and mammals. It is known from a few skeletons collected in Greenland earlier this century. Although Greenland is cold now, it was quite a warm place in the Late Devonian since it lay fairly close to the equator (*see p.12*). *Ichthyostega* had four legs, instead of fins, so it obviously walked on land. Also, it did not have fishy gills. However, it still has some fishlike features which show its ancestry; the tail has a broad tail fin at the end, and the head is low and streamlined, as in a swimming animal. *Ichthyostega* could probably move about slowly on land, but it still fed on fish in the water.

KAMPTOBAATAR

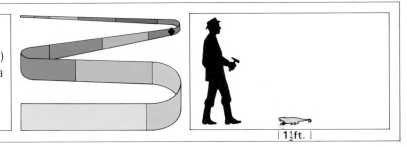

> KAMP-to-BA-tar
? Bend (mammal from Ulan) Batar (Mongolia)
ⓝ Z. Kielen-Jaworowska (1970)
ⓛ Mongolia
◆ Cretaceous

1½ft.

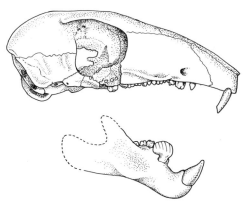

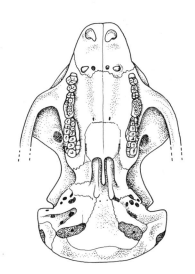

Kamptobaatar skull, side (*above*) and bottom (*below*) view showing dental formation.

The mammals that lived during the age of the mammals are generally poorly known. This is partly because most of them, like *Morganucodon*, were small, and also because they seem to have been quite rare. Some remarkable new discoveries in the deserts of Mongolia have now shown what some of these primitive mammals looked like in detail. *Kamptobaatar* is only the size of a small mouse, but the skull is almost perfectly preserved. The snout is quite short, and it bears two main types of teeth: a pair of long chisellike teeth at the front which were probably used for gnawing wood or tough plants, and three or four long teeth covered in bumps, which were used to grind up the food. This arrangement of teeth, and the skull shape, are like those of rodents such as rats and mice, but *Kamptobaatar* belongs to a more primitive group that was important during the last parts of the age of the dinosaurs, and survived well into the age of the mammals, with forms like *Ptilodus*. These were the first successful plant-eating mammals.

KANNEMEYERIA

> KAN-ah-MAY-er-ee-a
? For Kannemeyer
Ⓝ H. G. Seeley (1909)
Ⓛ South Africa India Tanzania
◆ Triassic

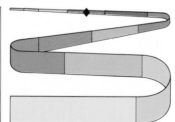

10ft.

The dicynodonts were one of the more successful groups of mammallike reptiles, being the main group of plant-eaters on land for the 30 million years before the dinosaurs came on the scene. In that time, they changed little, from the early *Dicynodon* to *Kannemeyeria*, which was a later form. It was as large as a hippopotamus, but even fatter, and its head was even bigger. The jaws were toothless, except for a pair of tusks, and it cut up its plant food with the sharpened jaw edges, just like those of a turtle. The high-crested skull bore strong muscles that moved the lower jaw in a powerful circular and back-and-forward kind of movement to cut up tough stems and roots. This heavily built animal was probably rather slow-moving since there were no meat-eaters around at the time that were big enough to attack it.

Kannemeyeria

KAYENTATHERIUM

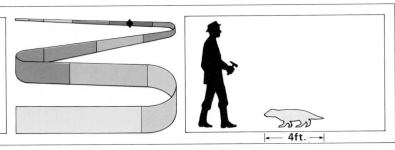

> ka-YENT-a-THEE-ree-um
? Kayenta beast
ⓝ H. D. Sues (1983)
Ⓘ Arizona
◆ Jurassic

— 4ft. —

Most of the mammallike reptiles died out in the Late Triassic, about 225 million years ago when the dinosaurs took over the earth. However, one line of mammallike reptiles survived through much of the Jurassic for another 60 million years. *Kayentatherium* is a typical large example, about the size of a labrador dog, known from much of the skeleton, and named in 1983. It has long gnawing teeth at the front of the mouth, and grinding cheek teeth behind, and evidently fed on tough plant material. In many respects, the teeth and jaws of *Kayentatherium* are like those of later primitive mammals such as *Kamptobaatar* and *Ptilodus*, or indeed true rodents such as rats or beavers.

KENNALESTES

> KEN-a-LES-teez
? McKenna's tooth
ⓝ Z. Kielen-Jaworowska (1969)
Ⓘ Mongolia
◆ Cretaceous

6 inches

One of the first placental mammals, the major group living today (*see p.90*), is *Kennalestes*. This is known from nearly complete skulls found in deposits in Mongolia. The teeth are all sharp, and *Kennalestes* must have fed on insects and other small animals. The teeth of *Kennalestes* also show that it was an early placental, but it is impossible to tell whether it is related to any of the modern groups of placental mammals.

Kennalestes skull

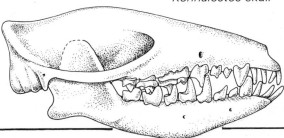

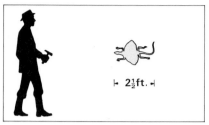

KUEHNEOSAURUS

> KOO-nee-oh-SAW-rus
? Kuehne's beast
ⓝ P. L. Robinson (1957)
ⓛ England
◆ Triassic

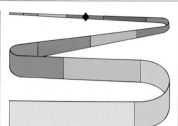

The kuehneosaurs of the Late Triassic were the third group of reptiles to conquer the air, after *Weigeltisaurus* in the Late Permian, and the pterosaurs, possibly in the Middle Triassic. These groups are all unrelated. *Kuehneosaurus* is known from several delicately preserved skeletons in the fossilized caves in southern England and Wales that produced *Clevosaurus* and *Morganucodon*, as well as from a close relative in the United States. *Kuehneosaurus* looks rather like some of the modern gliding lizards that live in tropical parts of the world, and use a thin sail of skin to glide from tree to tree. *Kuehneosaurus* had a normal lizardlike body, although it probably is not a true lizard, and enormously long ribs that stick out at the side. In life these were covered with skin, and *Kuehneosaurus* could glide for many tens of yards among the tree tops in search of insect food.

Kuehneosaurus

LAGOSUCHUS

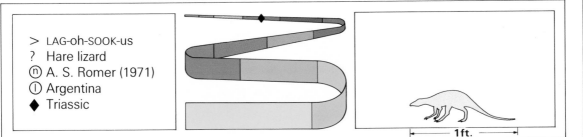

> LAG-oh-SOOK-us
? Hare lizard
Ⓝ A. S. Romer (1971)
Ⓘ Argentina
◆ Triassic

1ft.

The dinosaurs, and possibly also the flying pterosaurs, arose from thecodontian ancestors such as *Ornithosuchus* and *Lagosuchus* at the end of the Middle Triassic, some 230 million years ago. *Lagosuchus* is an important "missing link" that looks like a tiny slender dinosaur in many respects — it was about the size and shape of a skinny rabbit — but still has some primitive features that show it is not yet a true dinosaur. Like the first dinosaurs, it ran about on its long hind legs. These were tucked right under the body instead of sprawling out at the side, as in the first thecodontians such as *Proterosuchus*. It was also bipedal, but its legs and hips were not as advanced as those of a true dinosaur.

LEPTICTIS

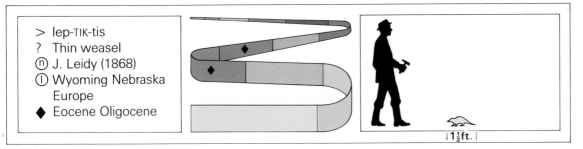

> lep-TIK-tis
? Thin weasel
Ⓝ J. Leidy (1868)
Ⓘ Wyoming Nebraska Europe
◆ Eocene Oligocene

1½ft.

The leptictids were a group of small insect-eating mammals that lived from 70 to 30 million years ago, and may form a link between early placentals such as *Kennalestes* and *Zalambdalestes*, and modern insectivores such as shrews and hedgehogs. *Leptictis* had a long snout and jaws lined with sharp little teeth, and it must have looked and lived rather like a hedgehog today. One of the problems in trying to decide on the relationships of *Leptictis* is that it is primitive in many respects, and shows no clear features that link it definitely with living groups.

LIMNOSCELIS

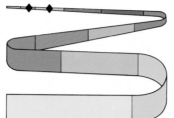

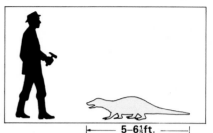

> LIM-no-SEEL-is
? Marsh scoundrel
(n) S. W. Williston (1911)
(l) Texas New Mexico
♦ Carboniferous Permian

5–6½ ft.

The dividing line between amphibians and reptiles is easy to see today: a frog is very different from a lizard or a crocodile! When the reptiles arose from the amphibians in the Carboniferous, there were several lines that could fall on either side of the divide. *Diadectes* and *Limnoscelis* are examples of animals that have been classified back and forward ever since they were first discovered, either as amphibians or as reptiles. They are generally placed on the amphibian side now. *Limnoscelis* was clearly a land-living animal with an advanced skull and with few specializations for swimming, so that it was nearly a reptile, and no one knows whether it laid eggs on land or in the water (*see p.140*). The snout is narrow, unlike the broad curve seen in typical early amphibians such as *Eryops* or *Eogyrinus*, and the long **daggerlike** teeth suggest that *Limnoscelis* may have fed on smaller **amphibians** and reptiles.

Limnoscelis

LIOPLEURODON

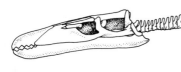

> LY-o-PLOO-ro-don
? Smooth-sided tooth
ⓝ Savage (1873)
ⓘ France
◆ Jurassic

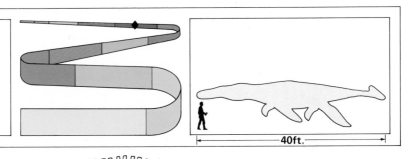

40ft.

Liopleurodon skeleton

A specialized side branch of the plesiosaurs were the pliosaurs, which lacked the long necks and small heads of *Elasmosaurus* or *Plesiosaurus*. *Liopleurodon*, like other typical pliosaurs, was a large animal with a massive skull, and it is likely that it fed on smaller plesiosaurs and ichthyosaurs, rather than fish. Apart from the head, the body, tail, and long swimming paddles are just like those of typical plesiosaurs.

LYCAENOPS

> ly-KINE-ops
? Wolf face
ⓝ R. Broom (1925)
ⓘ South Africa
◆ Permian

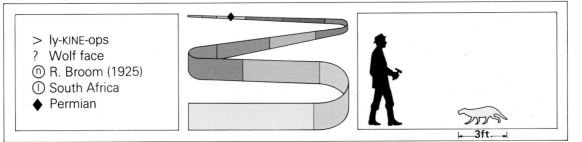

3ft.

During the heyday of the mammal-like reptiles, in the Late Permian, the most successful meat-eaters were the gorgonopsians such as *Lycaenops*. This dog-sized animal had powerful legs for fast running, a flexible body, and a fairly long neck. The skull had a long snout, a small number of sharp teeth for cutting meat, and a pair of large fangs for piercing the thick skin of the plant-eating mammal-like reptiles, such as *Dicynodon*, which it ate. Its legs were not so well adapted for running as those of a dog: they stuck out sideways in a sprawling posture, but *Lycaenops* was fast enough to capture the piglike dicynodonts.

EVOLUTION OF THE MAMMALS

The mammals arose some 220 million years ago, not long after the dinosaurs came to prominence. For the next 160 million years, the mammals remained as small secretive animals that crept out to catch insects and collect nuts and berries at night. They could live like this at night because they had warm blood and a covering of hair over their bodies which kept them warm after the sun had set.

The Jurassic and Cretaceous mammals include a great range of small to cat-sized animals such as *Kamptobaatar, Morganucodon*, and *Sinoconodon*. The ancestors of the three modern groups of mammals also emerged in the Cretaceous. The three groups are the monotremes, including the duck-billed platypus which lays eggs, the marsupials, like koalas and kangaroos which carry their babies in a pouch, and the placentals, which are all of the other mammals.

When the dinosaurs died out, 66 million years ago, the placental mammals seemed to evolve very rapidly. All of the great range of modern groups — from mice to elephants, and from whales to bats — emerged within the first 10 million years of the Cenozoic Era. The exact pattern of this rapid evolution is very hard to make out from the fossil record because things were happening so quickly. Some of these early mammals include forms like *Arctocyon, Hyopsodus, Oxyaena,* and *Purgatorius*, some of which were ancestral to living mammals, such as ourselves, and some of which belong to groups that soon died out.

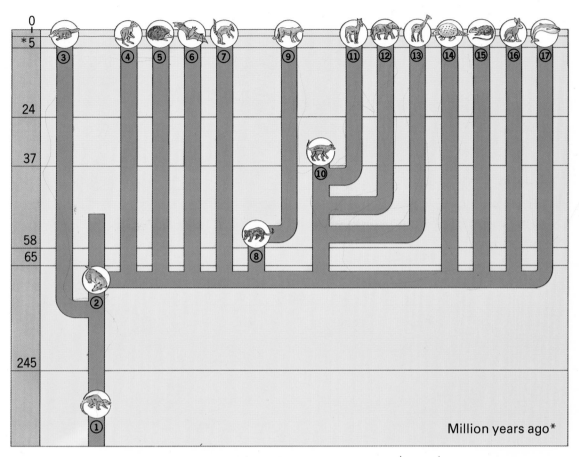

0
*5

24

37

58
65

245

Million years ago*

③ ④ ⑤ ⑥ ⑦ ⑨ ⑪ ⑫ ⑬ ⑭ ⑮ ⑯ ⑰

⑩

⑧

②

①

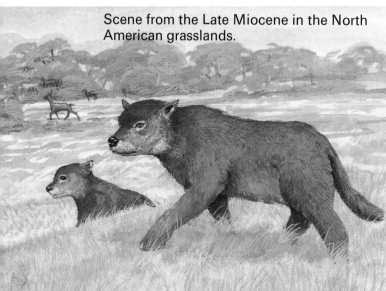

Scene from the Late Miocene in the North American grasslands.

Key to mammalian evolution

1 Mammal like reptiles
2 Mesozoic mammals
3 Monotremes
4 Marsupials
5 Insectivores
6 Bats
7 Primates
8 Creodonts
9 Carnivores
10 Condylarths
11 Horses, rhinoceroces
12 Elephants
13 Pigs, cows, deer
14 Anteaters, sloths
15 Rodents
16 Rabbits, hares
17 Whales, dolphins

MACRAUCHENIA

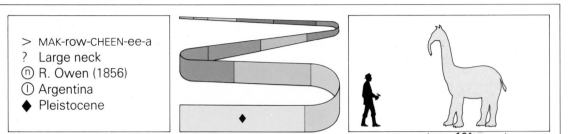

> MAK-row-CHEEN-ee-a
? Large neck
ⓝ R. Owen (1856)
ⓘ Argentina
◆ Pleistocene

◆

⊢—10ft.—⊣

The mammals evolved in isolation in South America during much of its history, and a variety of "mimics" arose, such as the elephantlike *Astrapotherium* and *Pyrotherium*, the piglike *Notostylops*, the camellike *Theosodon*, and the hippopotamuslike *Toxodon*. *Macrauchenia* did not look like any familiar animal; it had the

Macrauchenia

body of a camel, but the trunk of an elephant. Although the trunk is not preserved as a fossil, there are large nostril openings on top of the skull, just like those of a modern elephant, which show that there must have been a fleshy trunk for sniffing out food, or danger, and possibly for picking up food. *Macrauchenia* had a long neck, and this suggests that it reached high into trees to find succulent leaves which it may have sucked together and grasped with its trunk. The legs were long, and *Macrauchenia* ran fast on its three-toed feet, probably in order to escape from catlike meat-eaters such as *Thylacosmilus*.

The first skeletons of *Macrauchenia* were found by Charles Darwin, the founder of evolutionary theory, when he visited Argentina in the 1830s. He thought that it was most like the living camels and llamas (llamas live today in South America), and it was only later that scientists realized that *Macrauchenia* was part of a unique group of placental mammals that evolved in South America and then died out in the last million years or so.

MAMMUTHUS

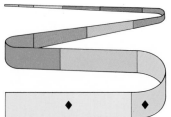

> MAM-uh-thus
? Burrower
ⓝ J. F. Blumenbach (1803)
Ⓛ Europe North America Africa
◆ Pliocene Pleistocene

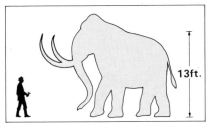

13ft.

The mammoth, *Mammuthus*, arose in Africa about five million years ago, and spread across Asia, Europe, and North America. The giant North American mammoth was the largest elephant of all time, reaching 13 feet at the shoulder. The most famous mammoth, the woolly mammoth of northern Europe and Russia was smaller than modern elephants, being 9 feet tall at the shoulder. Dozens of specimens have been dug up from the frozen soil of eastern Russia where whole bodies were deep-frozen for tens of thousands of years. The flesh of these woolly mammoths is still apparently edible!

Mammuthus

MEGALOCEPHALUS

> MEG-al-oh-SEF-al-us
? Great head
ⓝ T. P. Barkas (1873)
Ⓛ North America
◆ Carboniferous

← 2½ft. →

Many of the Carboniferous amphibians seem to have lived in and around the warm coal swamp ponds of Europe and North America. *Megalocephalus* is known from some good skull remains, but almost nothing is known of its skeleton. The skull is long, and the jaws lined with sharp crocodilelike teeth which were presumably used to capture fish.

Megalocephalus skull

MEGALOCEROS

> MEG-al-O-ser-os
? Great horn
ⓝ J. F. Blumenbach (1803)
Ⓛ Ireland Germany China
◆ Pleistocene

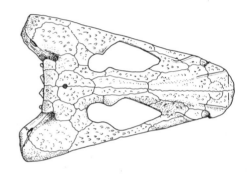

5ft.

The Giant Irish deer, *Megaloceros*, was one of the most striking large mammals of Europe. It spread much farther than Ireland, reaching as far east as Russia and China.

Megaloceros is famous for its enormous antlers which reached a span of 12 feet in the largest male specimens. In modern deer, the antlers are used by males in fighting for mates. In *Megaloceros*, the antlers reached an unbelievably huge size, and they must have been a great burden for the older animals to carry around. *Megaloceros* died out about 12,000 years ago, when the last ice retreated from Europe, but some may have lived on in Austria until 500 B.C.

MEGATHERIUM

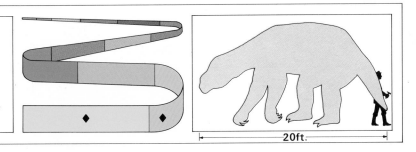

> MEG-a-THEE-ree-um
? Great beast
ⓝ R. Owen (1856)
ⓛ Argentina
◆ Pliocene Pleistocene

20ft.

Some of the strangest mammals in South America today are the tree sloths which spend their time moving slowly through the trees, and hanging upside down beneath the branches, feeding on leaves. From about 35 million years ago, there were some much larger sloths, the ground sloths, which achieved some success, and great size by the Pleistocene. *Megatherium* is the best-known large ground sloth since dozens of complete skeletons have been dug up. The first specimen to be seen by scientists was sent to Spain by the governor of Buenos Aires in Brazil in 1789. The skeleton showed that an animal as large as an elephant had once lived in South America, but had been a very different shape.

Megatherium could walk about on all fours in a fairly slow fashion but it could also stand up on its hind legs. It had a vast hip girdle, and broad short tail, so that when it reared up, the tail helped to form a kind of firm supporting tripod together with the two legs. The deep jaws probably housed a long tongue, as in the tree sloths, which may have been used to seize leaves.

Megatherium reared up to reach into the tops of trees, and it used the long claws on its hands to gather leaves together. Relatives of *Megatherium* spread over much of the southern United States, but the whole group died out some 11,000 years ago.

Megatherium

MERYCHIPPUS

> MER-ee-KIP-us
? Part horse
ⓝ J. Leidy (1856)
ⓘ Oregon California
   Texas
◆ Miocene Pliocene

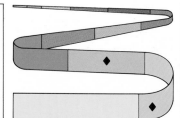

3ft.

Merychippus

The evolution of the horses, from tiny *Hyracotherium* to the modern forms, took a long time, and followed many side branches. The first horse that probably looked similar to a small modern pony was *Merychippus*. It had long legs for fast running, and it had a single functioning toe, the hoof, on each foot. It really still had three toes on each foot, a primitive feature, but two of them were very short and small, and did not reach the ground. In addition, there were major changes in the jaws and teeth. Until that time, the earlier horses had fed mainly on leaves from trees and bushes. Then, about 15 million years ago, they switched to grass. The great warm forests of the early parts of the age of the mammals were dying back and prairies of grass were spreading over North America, Europe, and Asia. Grass is much tougher than tree leaves since it contains silica, the main ingredient of sand, and silica wears teeth down quickly. *Merychippus* was the first horse to have modern teeth that could cope with silica. These teeth are deep-rooted and grow continuously to keep up with the wear, and they have a complex pattern of folded dentine, enamel and cement to give a tough grinding surface. *Merychippus* had a long "horsey" face, unlike that of *Hyracotherium*, in order to hold the new tougher teeth.

MERYCOIDODON

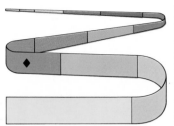

> MER-ee-KOID-o-don
? Ruminant form tooth
ⓝ J. Leidy (1848)
ⓘ Nebraska South
  Dakota
◆ Oligocene

|← 4ft. →|

The oreodonts, such as *Merycoidodon*, were a successful group of piglike plant-eaters for about 30 million years in North America. They had short legs with four toes on each foot, so they fall in the "even-toed" group of plant-eaters, but it is not certain whether they are related more closely to modern pigs or camels. The toes and fingers bore narrow curved claws, rather than hooves, and it has even been suggested that the oreodonts climbed trees, although there is no evidence that they could grasp branches. Long legs and hooves evolved only later among plant-eating mammals such as deer and horses allowing them to run fast. The oreodonts were probably slow-moving animals that fed quietly among the trees, and never needed to run fast. The head is short and the teeth are mixed, like those of a pig; short sharp teeth at the front for cropping plant food, fairly long fangs, and broad grinding cheek teeth at the back. Large herds of *Merycoidodon* must have moved through the American mid-west 30 million years ago since fossil collectors have found enormous deposits containing thousands of skeletons.

Merycoidodon

MESONYX

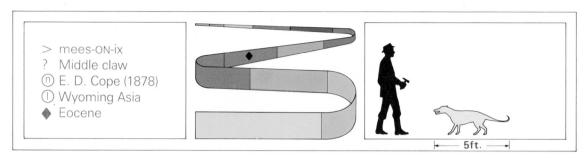

- > mees-ON-ix
- ? Middle claw
- ⓝ E. D. Cope (1878)
- ⓛ Wyoming Asia
- ◆ Eocene

5ft.

When the mammals started to take over the earth 65 million years ago, there were no large meat-eaters. Large birds such as *Diatryma* and *Phorusrhacos* took on this job in some parts of the world, while in others, strange doglike animals arose. *Mesonyx* was about the size of a sheep, but it had a vaguely doglike skull armed with good meat-cutting teeth.

Mesonyx, although smaller than its giant relative *Andrewsarchus*, was still no doubt able to tackle most of the small and medium-sized plant-eaters of its day, including the horse *Hyracotherium* or the condylarths *Hyopsodus* and *Phenacodus*.

MESOSAURUS

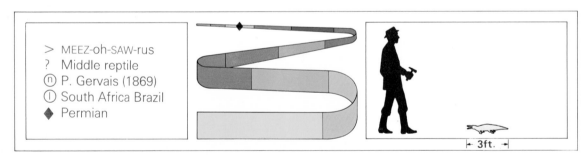

- > MEEZ-oh-SAW-rus
- ? Middle reptile
- ⓝ P. Gervais (1869)
- ⓛ South Africa Brazil
- ◆ Permian

3ft.

The first reptile to adapt to life in the sea was *Mesosaurus*, a tiny animal with no obvious close relatives. The jaws are lined with long narrow teeth that may have been used to strain tiny shrimps from the water as it swam about.

Mesosaurus

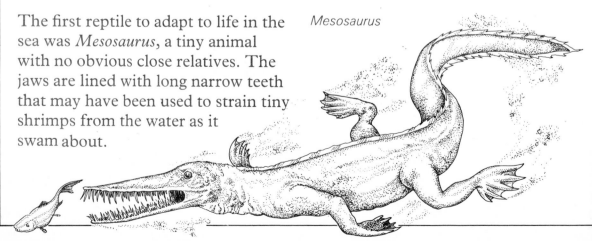

METOPOSAURUS

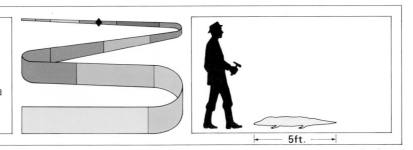

> me-TOPE-o-SAW-rus
? Forehead reptile
Ⓝ F. Fraas (1889)
Ⓛ India Germany Africa
◆ Triassic

⊢— 5ft. —⊣

The primitive amphibian types mainly died out during the Permian period, but a few lines were moderately successful in the Triassic, and some even survived beyond that time into the age of the dinosaurs. The metoposaurs lived at the same time as the plagiosaurs like *Gerrothorax*, and they seem to have been quite successful. Dozens of specimens of *Metoposaurus* have been found in Germany, the United States, and India. It seems that large colonies of this animal lived in lakes which may have dried out from time to time, killing off many animals that depended on the fish.

   The skull of *Metoposaurus* is low and has a broad rounded outline as in its distant ancestors from the Carboniferous and Permian, such as *Eryops* and *Greererpeton*. The nostrils are large, and the small eye sockets are placed well forward. A striking feature on the top of the skull of *Metoposaurus* is the network of broad grooves that wind along each side in a double row. These grooves lay just below the surface of the skin when the animal was alive, and they are

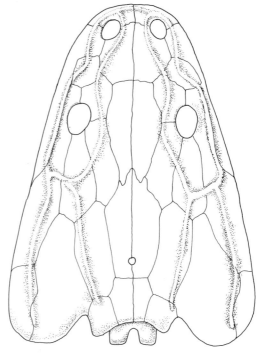

Metoposaurus skull

probably equivalent to the lateral line system of living fishes. This contains specialized nerves that allow fishes to pick up weak electrical signals or movements in the water nearby. Even if it is impossible to see through muddy water, a fish can sense another animal nearby using its lateral line, and it is likely that *Metoposaurus* could do the same. Other early amphibians also had this system.

MIXOSAURUS

> MIX-oh-SAW-rus
? Mixed reptile
(n) G. Baur (1887)
(l) France Germany
China Norway New
Zealand
◆ Triassic

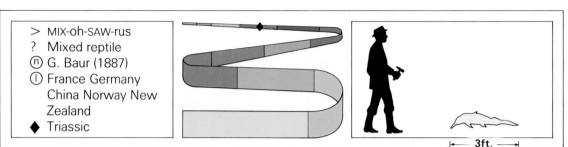

3ft.

Early Triassic ichthyosaurs such as *Grippia* show a number of primitive features that hark back to their land-living ancestors, but *Mixosaurus*, only five million years or so later, was a fully efficient dolphinlike swimmer. At first sight, *Mixosaurus* seems like its later relatives such as *Ichthyosaurus* and *Ophthalmosaurus*, but it is thinner-bodied, the paddles are not so large, and the end of the backbone in the tail is not bent down so sharply. *Mixosaurus* has been found all over the world, and it was clearly able to swim in the shallow waters of all parts of the world from north to south. The best specimens of this relatively small ichthyosaur come from quarries of high quality slate in the alpine region of central Europe.

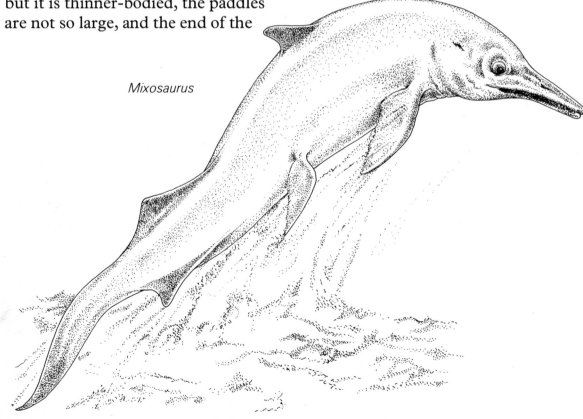

Mixosaurus

MOERITHERIUM

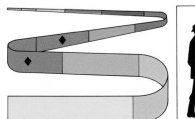

- > MER-ih-THEE-ree-um
- ? Part mammal
- Ⓝ C. W. Andrews (1906)
- Ⓛ Senegal Mali
- ◆ Eocene Oligocene

3ft.

Moeritherium

For a long time *Moeritherium* has been regarded as the oldest known elephant, but even older remains were reported in 1984 from Algeria. These are much less complete than the specimens of *Moeritherium*, some of which came from the same beds in Egypt that produced *Aegyptopithecus* and *Arsinotherium*. *Moeritherium* probably looked like a pigmy hippopotamus, and lacked tusks and a trunk. The cheek teeth and other features of the skull and skeleton show that it is an early elephant, but probably a side branch from the line to modern forms. *Moeritherium* has long front teeth in the upper and lower jaws which stick forward, rather like the double sets of tusks in the later gomphotheres such as *Gomphotherium*. The fossils of *Moeritherium* come from rocks laid down in the mouth of a river near the sea, so it may have lived largely in the water, and scraped up water plants with its shovel teeth.

MORGANUCODON

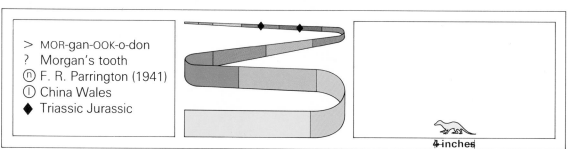

> MOR-gan-OOK-o-don
? Morgan's tooth
Ⓝ F. R. Parrington (1941)
Ⓛ China Wales
♦ Triassic Jurassic

4 inches

The oldest mammals date from the Late Triassic, some 215 million years ago, but they are known only from a few samples of fossilized teeth. The first reasonably well-known fossil mammal is *Morganucodon* from fossilized cave deposits in south Wales, as well as from China. *Morganucodon* was about the size of a mouse, although it had a longer body and a shorter tail. The long narrow snout bears small sharp teeth of the sort used to capture and crush insects and other small animals. The eyes are large, so *Morganucodon* probably hunted its prey at night, moving rapidly among the roots of trees and through the litter of leaves and twigs on the floor of the forest. The hands and feet have long claws which could be used to grasp branches or insect prey. It is likely that *Morganucodon* had a warm body temperature, but it probably continued to lay eggs, as some primitive mammals still do today (*see p.90*).

MOROPUS

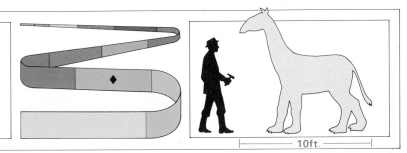

> mor-OH-pus
? Foolish foot
(n) J. Leidy (1873)
(l) Nebraska California
◆ Miocene

10ft.

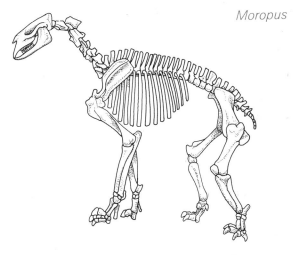

Moropus

The oddest relatives of the horses and rhinoceroses, the living "odd-toed" plant-eaters, were the chalicotheres, such as *Chalicotherium* and *Moropus*. *Moropus*, at 10 feet long, was by far the largest, being as big as a horse. The group is characterized by the arms being longer than the legs, and both hands and feet had strange split claws that could be drawn back into the fleshy part of the foot like a cat's claw. *Moropus* fed on leaves, as is shown by the horselike skull and the teeth, which are like those of early horses such as *Hyracotherium*. However, it seems that the chalicotheres may have had other abilities that assisted them in finding untapped sources of food. The strange shape of the body has suggested to scientists recently that *Moropus* may have reared up on its hind legs and torn branches and stems from trees with its strange, powerful, gorillalike arms.

In a way, the chalicotheres may have been like the South American ground sloths such as *Megatherium* which also sat up on its hind legs and used its arms to collect plant food.

The hind part of the skeleton of *Moropus* supports this hypothesis. The legs are short and stocky, the tail is short, and the hip girdle is broad and bowllike, the right shape for supporting a heavy body as it rears up. Some North American relatives of *Moropus* had thick bone in the roof of the skull which suggests that the males may have butted their heads together during fights for mates. There are no horns or antlers, but the head-butting displays of these modern forms mean that they had thick skulls so they did not kill each other during contests.

MOSASAURUS

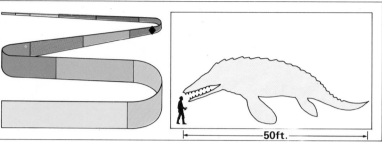

> MOSE-a SAW-rus
? Meuse reptile
ⓝ W. D. Conybeare (1822)
ⓘ Africa New Jersey France Sweden
◆ Cretaceous

50ft.

The mosasaurs were a highly successful group of fish-eating reptiles that diversified in the Late Cretaceous seas, at a time when the ichthyosaurs had died out and the plesiosaurs were in decline. *Mosasaurus* had a long slender body with a deep flat-sided tail which was used to power its swimming. The hands and feet were modified to paddles, probably used in steering, and the long powerful jaws were lined with broad sharp teeth. These were used for piercing the shells of ammonites, coiled swimming shellfish that were common at the time; this is known because ammonite shells have been found with lines of tooth holes made by a mosasaur. The odd thing is that the giant mosasaurs were lizards, related closely to the living monitor lizards!

Mosasaurus

MOSCHOPS

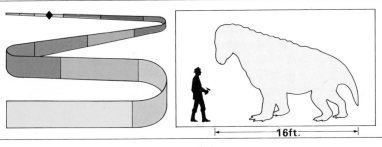

> MOS-kops
? Calf eye
ⓝ R. Broom (1911)
ⓛ South Africa Russia
◆ Permian

16ft.

Moschops

Among the mammallike reptiles of the Late Permian were many odd forms, such as *Estemmenosuchus* and its close relative *Moschops*. *Moschops* was a massive animal, as large as an ox, and yet probably much heavier and slower moving. It had a barrellike rib cage, which suggests that it had a large digestive system to deal with poor quality plant food. The blunt teeth and deep jaws also point to a diet of tough plants. The shoulder girdle and hip girdle were heavy, and the arms and legs rather short and the hands and feet small, so that it could only have taken short strides despite its great body size. The front quarters are in fact higher than the hind quarters, which seems at first to be similar to the much later chalicothere mammals, *Chalicotherium* and *Moropus*. However, it is most unlikely that *Moropus* could rear up on its hind legs and use its arms to gather food. The massive high shoulders may have had more to do with fighting in *Moschops*. It has a very thick skull roof, with about 4 inches of bone, and it seems likely that male *Moschops* had head-butting contests as wild sheep and goats do today.

NEANDERTHAL MAN

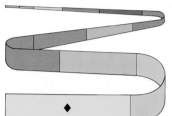 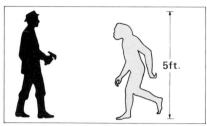

> NEE-an-der-TAL man
? Neander valley man
ⓝ H. Schaafhaysen (1857)
Ⓛ Germany France Austria Turkey
◆ Pleistocene

5ft.

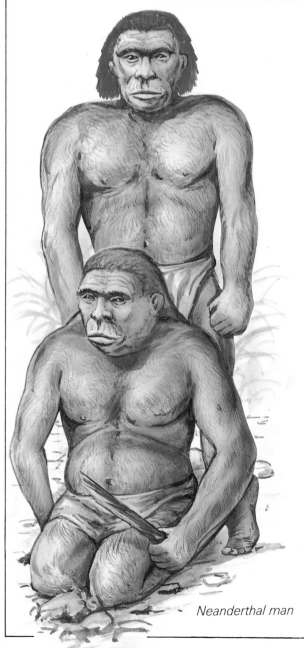

Neanderthal man

Neanderthal man first came to light in 1857 when a skeleton was found in the Neander Valley in Germany. At first it was thought to be the remains of a Russian soldier trapped while fleeing from the approach of Napoleon's troops around 1800. It was soon realized that the skeleton was thousands of years old, and that it represented an extinct human race.

More recent studies have shown that the 1857 skeleton was an old man, crippled with arthritis. Other fossils of younger Neanderthal people show that they were more heavily built than we are, but that they had larger brains! The skull had prominent bulges over the eyebrows and a heavy jaw. The Neanderthals were advanced enough to bury their dead which is why there are so many plentiful remains available to palaeontologists. Their stocky body was adapted for life in the cold of the last Ice Ages, during which they lived in caves, and the Neanderthal race of Europe gave way to fully modern human races after the ice retreated during which time the species may have overlapped.

106

NECROLESTES

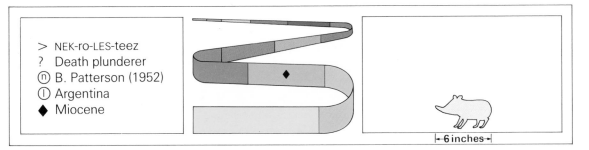

> NEK-ro-LES-teez
? Death plunderer
ⓝ B. Patterson (1952)
① Argentina
◆ Miocene

|←6 inches→|

Sometimes the study of fossils is very frustrating! A specimen is found that is so unusual that it is known to belong to a unique kind of animal, but there is so little preserved that we cannot find out the whole story of what it looked like, or exactly how it lived. *Necrolestes* is such a case. A single fossil snout of this creature is known, but this unpromising fragment is so strange, that it has been placed in its own group. The teeth are those of an insect-eater and marsupial. *Necrolestes* was no larger than a shrew and an unusual feature is that the snout curves upward and there are very large nostrils. As in other insect-eaters, *Necrolestes* probably had a good sense of smell which helped it to find its prey, and the upturned snout may have improved this sense greatly.

NEOTHERIUM

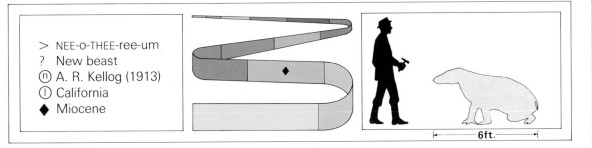

> NEE-O-THEE-ree-um
? New beast
ⓝ A. R. Kellog (1913)
① California
◆ Miocene

|← 6ft. →|

The seals, sealions, and walruses of today are well adapted to life in the sea, and yet they show clear similarities to their land-living relatives, dogs and bears. One of the oldest walruses, *Neotherium*, was smaller than living forms, and it did not have the long tusks that modern forms use to scrape shellfish from rocks. Male *Neotherium* were already larger than the females, a feature of the group since the males fight each other for mates and use their size to threaten each other.

NOTHOSAURUS

> NOTHE-oh-SAW-rus
? Spurious reptile
ⓝ G. von Muenster (1834)
ⓛ Germany South Africa
◆ Triassic

10ft.

The seas of Triassic times saw many swimming fish-eating reptiles, such as *Askeptosaurus*, the ichthyosaurs *Grippia* and *Mixosaurus*, *Placodus*, and *Tanystropheus*. Another successful group were the nothosaurs, which ranged from lizard-sized to 13 feet long. Large collections of well-preserved skeletons have been found in central Europe. These show that *Nothosaurus* had a long neck, a long low skull with sharp teeth for piercing fish, a narrow tail, and broad flat paddlelike limbs. *Nothosaurus* used its arms and legs in swimming, but this may have been by a kind of "doggy paddle." At the end of the Triassic, the nothosaurs may have given rise to the plesiosaurs, which were much more highly adapted to life in the sea, but this is not certain.

Nothosaurus

NOTHROTHERIUM

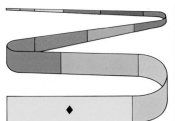

> NOTH-ro-THEE-ree-um
? Sluggish beast
ⓝ R. Lydekker (1894)
① Argentina
◆ Pleistocene

6ft.

The ground sloths of South America, such as *Megatherium*, were able to enter North America when a land bridge formed across Panama in Central America some three million years ago. The best-known North American ground sloth, *Nothrotherium* spread over much of the southwestern United States. *Nothrotherium* died out as little as 11,000 years ago, and some of the cave deposits preserve "soft" remains such as hair and droppings. The hair is yellowish in color, while the dung contains seeds and twigs of desert plants. When the large ground sloths died out, possibly as a result of hunting by humans, no other animal was able to take over this diet of unpromising plant food.

NOTOSTYLOPS

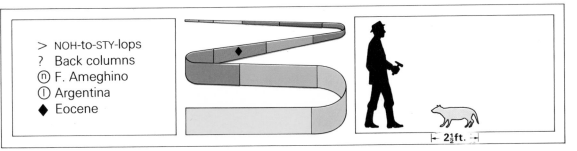

> NOH-to-STY-lops
? Back columns
ⓝ F. Ameghino
① Argentina
◆ Eocene

2½ft.

The plant-eaters of South America included a variety of animals such as *Astrapotherium*, *Macrauchenia*, and *Pyrotherium*, which belonged to unique groups that lived nowhere else. One of the primitive members of the main group is *Notostylops*, a sheeplike animal that had strong grinding teeth and a deep jaw. However, unlike sheep, it still had long nipping teeth at the front which may have been used to pierce tough leaves or fruits. These South American plant-eaters are all grouped together because they share special characteristics of their teeth, and because of additional cavities in the braincase on either side of the middle ear which may have given them a specially good sense of hearing.

OPHIDERPETON

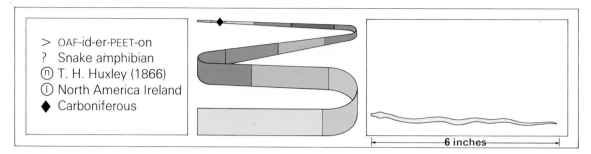

> OAF-id-er-PEET-on
? Snake amphibian
ⓝ T. H. Huxley (1866)
ⓛ North America Ireland
◆ Carboniferous

6 inches

Some of the Carboniferous amphibians were very different from the typical heavily built fish-eaters such as *Crassigyrinus*, *Eogyrinus* or *Greererpeton*. A few lines evolved into small salamanderlike forms, although they are not related to modern salamanders, and some of those became very odd in appearance, such as *Diplocaulus*. Others, which may be related, actually lost their limbs altogether, and became snake-like.

Ophiderpeton is an example of this group. This tiny animal probably looked like a worm in life, but its skeleton suggests that it may be derived from some form like *Greererpeton*. The tiny body contained as many as 230 vertebrae, instead of the typical 50 or so, and all traces of the arms and legs have been lost.

There is no doubt that the ancestors of *Ophiderpeton* had legs, but it must have had no need for them at all in its life of swimming in ponds, or inching through the leaf litter in the forest floor in search of small insects to eat. The head is one of the most remarkable features of the

group, being a narrow cylinder that has become simplified compared to most other amphibians of its day. It is so small that many of the skull bones have disappeared, or they may have fused with others. The nostrils and eyes are large, so it had a good sense of smell and of sight, possibly to find its prey. The jaw is weak and could not deal with tough food.

Ophthalmosaurus

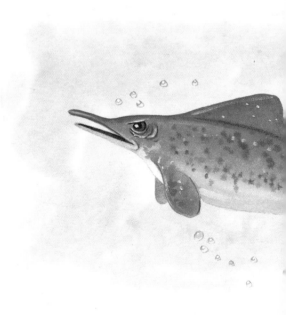

OPHTHALMOSAURUS

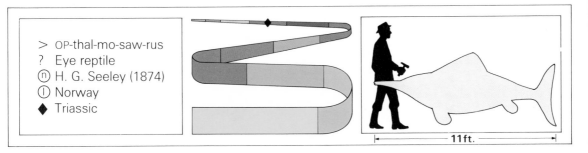

> OP-thal-mo-saw-rus
? Eye reptile
ⓝ H. G. Seeley (1874)
ⓛ Norway
◆ Triassic

11ft.

Many of the later ichthyosaurs became quite large, some as large as whales. *Ophthalmosaurus* was bigger than typical Triassic forms such as *Grippia* and *Mixosaurus*, and it shows advances in several features. The head is roughly the same as that of the slightly older *Ichthyosaurus*, but the paddles are even more modified away from the primitive form. For example, the thigh bone and the shin bones in the hind paddle have become round disks of bone, and they are hard to distinguish from the other bones of the paddle. The hind paddle is considerably smaller than the fore paddle. The bones in most of the front paddle are derived from the normal finger bones found in all land vertebrates, but there are many more of them. Whereas most land vertebrates have four or five short bones in each finger, *Ophthalmosaurus*, and other later ichthyosaurs, often have as many as 20 or 25. Some forms may have extra side fingers, to widen the paddles.

ORNITHOSUCHUS

> OR-nith-oh-SOOK-us
? Bird lizard
ⓝ E. T. Newton (1893)
ⓛ Scotland
◆ Triassic

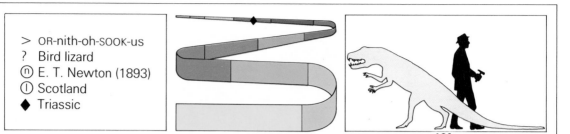

13ft.

Dinosaurs arose about 230 million years ago as small meat-eating animals that ran on their hind legs. Their ancestors are called thecodontians, and that group includes a variety of forms from the primitive *Proterosuchus* and *Erythrosuchus*, to the active *Parasuchus*, *Stagonolepis* and *Ticinosuchus*, which lay on the line to crocodiles, and *Euparkeria*, *Ornithosuchus* and *Lagosuchus*, which lay on the line to the dinosaurs. *Ornithosuchus* was a moderate-sized meat-eater that fed on other smaller thecodontians, rhynchosaurs such as *Hyperodapedon*, and mammallike reptiles such as *Diademodon*. It looks pretty much like a dinosaur already, but it does not have the fully advanced upright posture of the hind legs. *Ornithosuchus* could probably run on its hind legs, but it walked on all fours most of the time.

Ornithosuchus

OXYAENA

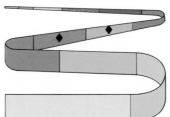

> OX-eye-EE-na
? Sharp hyena
ⓝ E. D. Cope (1874)
① Colorado Wyoming
  France
◆ Paleocene Eocene

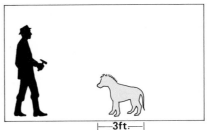

⊢ **3ft.** ⊣

The main meat-eating mammals in the early parts of the age of the mammals were creodonts such as *Hyaenodon* and *Oxyaena*. These animals probably looked rather like modern hunting cats and dogs, but they are not directly related to such modern forms. The creodonts were much more primitive in a variety of features. For example, their legs were shorter, which meant that they could not have run as fast as the modern meat-eaters, and their wrists and claws were less advanced. Creodont claws were curious cleft hooflike structures that were presumably covered by a horn sheath in life, just like the claws of modern meat-eaters. There were also five fingers in the hand and five toes in the foot, a primitive character compared to modern cats and dogs which have only four. In addition, the creodonts probably had a poorer sense of hearing.

Oxyaena has a short-snouted rather catlike skull with long fangs for piercing flesh, and specially modified cheek teeth which have a broadly triangular pointed shape for cutting

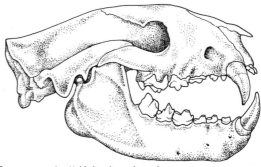

Oxyaena skull (9 inches long)

flesh or cracking bones. The body is long and flexible, and the tail is long. The short legs and flat feet were more adapted for moving about rapidly in a forest, slinking in and out of the trees, rather than for galloping across open grassland.

Oxyaena and its close relatives are known only from the Paleocene and Eocene of North America and Europe where they hunted smaller plant-eaters such as *Hyopsodus*, *Hyracotherium* and *Pantolambda*. Larger prey was left to the mesonychids such as *Mesonyx* and *Andrewsarchus*. Although *Oxyaena* was no larger than a modern North American wolverine, it had some relatives that were as large as bears.

PAKICETUS

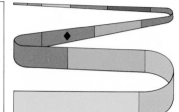

> PAK-i-SEET-us
? Pakistan whale
(n) P. D. Gingerich and D. E. Russell (1981)
(!) Pakistan
◆ Eocene

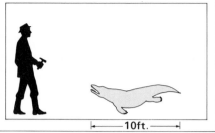

|← 10ft. →|

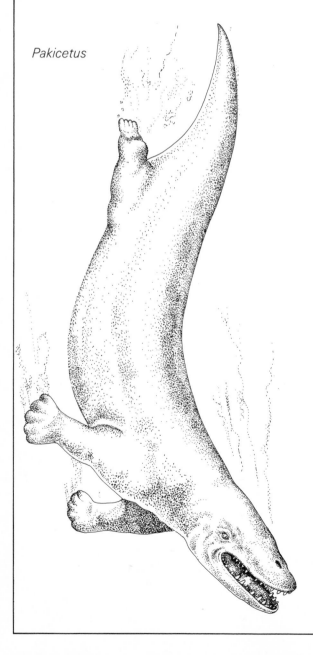

Pakicetus

Until recently the oldest-known whales were animals such as *Basilosaurus*, which were very large and quite unlike their land-living ancestors. A much older whale, *Pakicetus*, was found in Pakistan in 1981, and it has given a great deal of information about how the whales orginated. Unfortunately, the remains of *Pakicetus* are rather sparse; there is only a braincase, some teeth, and parts of the lower jaw. These are enough, however, to show that it is a whale. The important thing is that the skull remains and the teeth show similarities to mesonychids such as *Mesonyx* and *Andrewsarchus*. So the whales probably arose from this group of heavy doglike meat-eaters.

Pakicetus was not completely adapted to living in the sea, as modern whales are. The structure of its ear shows that it could hear best in the air rather than underwater. The reconstruction of *Pakicetus* shown here is largely guesswork since only the skull is known. It is given "paddle legs" like those of a seal since it almost certainly moved about on land as well as in the sea.

PALAEOCASTOR

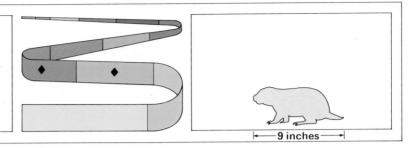

9 inches

Beavers today are well known for the way in which they build dams from trees. They build cozy living chambers within these dams, and may burrow into the soil. *Palaeocastor* was a remarkable beaver that specialized in burrowing. For years geologists had been puzzled by huge corkscrewlike structures that ran as deep as 8 feet in fossil soils and sands of Nebraska. These turned out to be burrows built by *Palaeocastor* as safe living chambers. The walls of the fossil burrows show scratch marks which match the long front teeth of *Palaeocastor*, so it dug by powerful scraping movements of the head, and then probably kicked the soil back with its feet. The vertical part of the burrow had a corkscrew shape, used like a spiral staircase. The animals lived in a flat burrow at the bottom which would have been warm and safe from meat-eaters.

Paleocastor

Palaeocastor burrow

PALAEOLAGUS

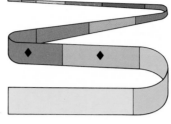

> PAL-ee-o-LAG-us
? Ancient hare
ⓝ J. Leidy (1856)
Ⓘ Nebraska South
  Dakota
◆ Oligocene Miocene

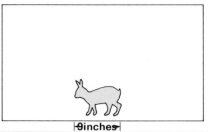

9inches

Modern rabbits and hares are common in nearly all parts of the world, and they are easy to identify, with their tall ears and long hind legs which are used in hopping or powerful running. In many ways they are like the rodents, such as rats, mice, and beavers. They have strong gnawing teeth at the front, short powerful jaws, and a fast rate of breeding. The origins of rabbits are, however, not so easy to trace. The best-known fossil rabbit is *Palaeolagus*, which is known from nearly complete skeletons. It is like the modern forms, and probably lived in the same way, feeding on grass and leaves, and living in shallow burrows.

PANTOLAMBDA

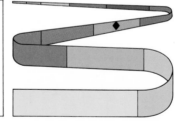

> PAN-to-LAM-da
? All lambda
ⓝ E. D. Cope (1882)
Ⓘ Wyoming
◆ Paleocene

3ft.

At the beginning of the age of mammals, some 60 million years ago, a number of rather short-lived groups came on the scene. The pantodonts, such as *Pantolambda*, were large pig- and hippolike plant-eaters that probably fed on roots and reedy plants around ponds. They were heavy slow-moving animals.

Pantolambda

PANTYLUS

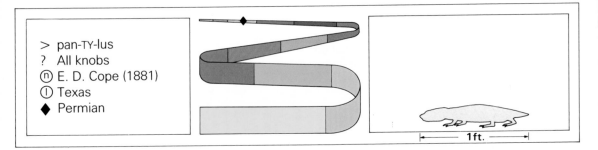

> pan-TY-lus
? All knobs
ⓝ E. D. Cope (1881)
ⓛ Texas
◆ Permian

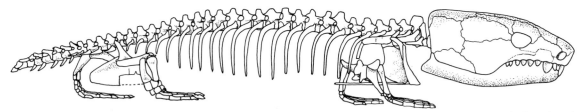

1 ft.

Pantylus skeleton (9 feet long)

The microsaurs were an unusual advanced group of early amphibians. Typical forms, including *Pantylus*, were small and probably looked a little like short-legged lizards. *Pantylus* had an unusually large head and the blunt rounded teeth may have been used to crush snails and other hard-bodied small animals. The microsaurs must have been rather slow moving since their legs are always quite short and sprawling. Some of them had long snakelike bodies, and they probably relied on their skill at hiding for protection. *Pantylus* and its relatives could have escaped the meat-eating sail-backed reptiles of the day, such as *Dimetrodon*, by hiding under rocks or in piles of fallen leaves.

The microsaurs were probably one of the first amphibian groups to live most of the time on land. Others also tried this new mode of life and some, like *Diadectes*, *Limnoscelis*, and *Seymouria* seem to have been close to the origin of the fully land-living reptiles. Some scientists have even thought that they were reptiles because of their adaptations for living on land. More usually, they are classified with the other small amphibian groups of the Carboniferous and Permian, animals like *Diplocaulus* and *Ophiderpeton*. Even this is not certain since these animals do not share any special features other than being small. The microsaurs seem to be related to the ancestors of frogs and salamanders, but no one can say how closely.

PARAMYS

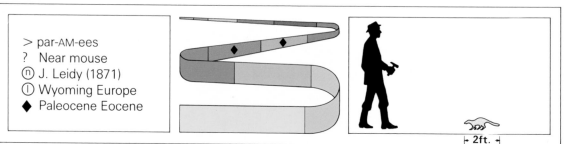

> par-AM-ees
? Near mouse
Ⓝ J. Leidy (1871)
Ⓛ Wyoming Europe
◆ Paleocene Eocene

├ 2ft. ┤

Paramys

The great mammal group of the rodents is probably the commonest on earth today, if one totals the numbers of mice and rats that live everywhere. However, the rodents are not the oldest modern mammal group since they arose only 55 million years ago. One of the first rodents was *Paramys*, a moderate-sized animal that probably looked a little like a squirrel. The body is long and flexible, and the long tail may well have had bushy hair in life. The hands and feet had long claws which could probably have been used in tree climbing.

Paramys shows primitive features in the teeth. Rodents probably owe their success to the pair of chisellike incisor teeth at the front; these are used to gnaw through wood and other tough plant materials, including wooden planks in houses and the wood and ropes of ships! *Paramys* had these remarkable teeth, but they were round instead of chisel-shaped, and they did not have the self-sharpening features of modern rodent teeth.

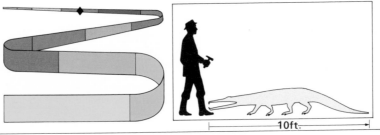

PARASUCHUS

> PAR-a-SOOK-us
? Near crocodile
ⓝ T. H. Huxley (1870)
ⓘ India
◆ Triassic

10ft.

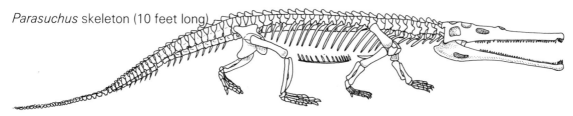

Parasuchus skeleton (10 feet long)

Phytosaurs such as *Parasuchus* became very common in the Late Triassic of Europe, North America, and India, and then died out. Although they look like crocodiles, with their long snouts and low armored bodies, close study shows that they are not related. They are related to animals such as *Stagonolepis* and *Ticinosuchus*, which lie on the line to crocodiles, but are much more primitive. *Parasuchus* could walk on land, but it moved faster in the water where it swam by beating its long powerful tail. The long jaws and sharp teeth show that it fed on fish.

PETROLACOSAURUS

> PET-rol-AK-o-SAW-rus
? Oil rock reptile
ⓝ P. D. Lane (1945)
ⓘ Kansas
◆ Carboniferous

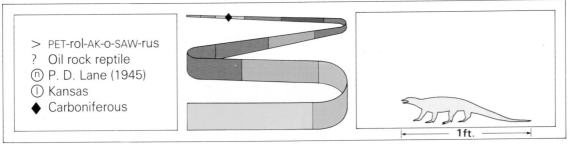

1ft.

Early in their history, the reptiles split into two major groups, one of which included the mammallike reptiles and led to the mammals, and the other (the diapsid reptiles) which includes the crocodiles, dinosaurs, lizards, and snakes, and led to the birds (*see p.140*). The first diapsid was *Petrolacosaurus*, an animal that probably looked like a long-legged, long-necked lizard. It is well known from a number of fossil skeletons.

PHENACODUS

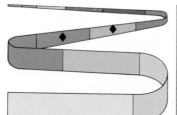

> FEN-a-KODE-us
? Impostor tooth
ⓝ E. D. Cope (1873)
Ⓛ Wyoming Colorado France
◆ Paleocene Eocene

5ft.

Phenacodus

If you had traveled back 60 million years to the Late Paleocene of North America, you might have seen small herds of an animal that looked rather like a horse. This was *Phenacodus*. It was about the size of a sheep, with short legs, a long low body, and a small head. Nevertheless, it had broad grinding teeth which show that it fed on plants, even though it is smaller and slower than a modern horse. *Phenacodus* was not a horse, although it may be close to the ancestry of early horses such as *Hyracotherium*. *Phenacodus* is generally placed in a group called the "condylarths" with forms such as *Hyopsodus*, and these animals are probably close to the origins of most of the larger plant-eating mammals today. *Phenacodus* is primitive in comparison with the true horses since it still has five fingers and five toes and it could bend its feet from side to side. This suggests that it could dodge rapidly in and out of the trees, and even climb a little, whereas true horses are adapted for fast running on the flat ground. In addition, *Phenacodus* had shorter legs than a horse and its tail is much longer, since it may have been used for balance. Finally, *Phenacodus* has a very small head with a tiny brain.

PHORUSRHACOS

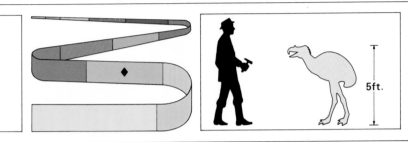

5ft.

The most successful large meat-eaters in South America for a long time were giant birds such as *Phorusrhacos*. This huge bird, nearly as tall as a grown human, had long powerful legs. These were adapted for fast running, and it could probably have kept pace with a modern race horse. *Phorusrhacos* had tiny wings that were not used in flight at all, but may have been used to keep balance. Its beak was massive, and probably strong enough to crack bones. It is likely that *Phorusrhacos* fed on the successful plant-eating mammals of South America, small relatives of *Notostylops*, *Theosodon*, and *Toxodon*. Relatives of *Phorusrhacos* lived on until about three million years ago, and some even crossed into North America. *Phorusrhacos* looks a little like *Diatryma*, but it seems that these two groups of giant meat-eating birds arose separately.

Phorusrhacos

PLACODUS

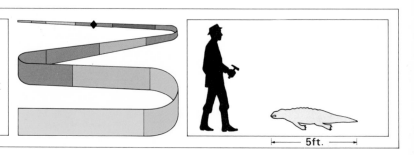

> PLAK-oh-DUS
? Plate tooth
ⓝ L. Agassiz (1833)
Ⓛ Germany South West Africa
◆ Triassic

5ft.

The placodonts, such as *Placodus*, were one of a number of reptile groups that conquered the seas in the Triassic. *Placodus* had a long bulky body and a long narrow tail. Its arms and legs were not really paddlelike, and were clearly still useful for walking on land. Under water, *Placodus* probably swam with a kind of doggy paddle. It did not need to be able to swim fast as the ichthyosaurs and plesiosaurs could, since its food did not move much. *Placodus* fed on oysters and other shellfish that were attached to underwater rocks. *Placodus* had broad jaws that bear four or five large flat teeth on each side used to crush shellfish.

PLESIADAPIS

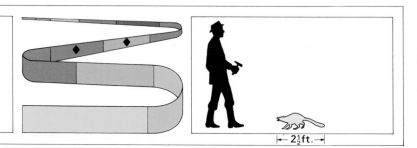

> PLEEZ-ee-AD-a-pis
? Near Adapis
ⓝ P. Gervais (1877)
Ⓛ Wyoming Colorado France Germany
◆ Paleocene Eocene

2½ft.

Humans, apes, and monkeys belong to the mammal order Primates. The oldest primate is *Purgatorius*, but the oldest primate skeleton belongs to a relative, *Plesiadapis*. In life, *Plesiadapis* probably looked like a cross between a squirrel and a monkey since it was a very primitive form. It had a long tail, strong grasping hands and feet armed with long claws, and a flexible body. All of these features show that it was an active tree-climber. The sharp teeth and good sense of smell suggest that *Plesiadapis* fed on insects. In addition, it had long front teeth and a gap behind which suggests a diet of fruit and leaves as well.

PLESIOSAURUS

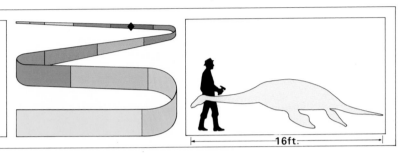

> PLEEZ-ee-oh-SAW-rus
? Ribbon reptile
ⓝ W. D. Conybeare (1821)
ⓛ Germany England
◆ Jurassic

16ft.

The first specimens of fossil reptiles to be seen by scientists may have been plesiosaurs. Fossil skeletons of *Plesiosaurus* itself came to light on the coasts of Yorkshire and Dorset in England, over 200 years ago, well before the first dinosaurs were recognized. Several fine skeletons were found between 1800 and 1820 by Mary Anning, the first professional fossil collector, and they caused a sensation when the scientists of her day in London and Bristol saw them. She was able to sell them to various British museums for huge sums of money. *Plesiosaurus* has a long neck and a small skull, as in more advanced relatives such as *Cryptocleidus* and *Elasmosaurus*. Its arms and legs are long paddles that were used to propel it through the water as it chased schools of fish.

Plesiosaurus

PLEUROSAURUS

> PLOO-roh-SAW-rus
? Rib reptile
ⓝ H. von Meyer (1831)
ⓛ Germany
◆ Jurassic Cretaceous

⊢ 2ft. ⊣

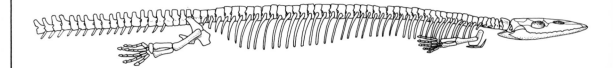

Pleurosaurus skeleton

The pleurosaurs were an unusual group of reptiles that took to the seas about 200 million years ago, and lived for some 75 million years. They fed on small fish side by side with the ichthyosaurs and plesiosaurs. *Pleurosaurus*, the best known example, has a long body with up to 57 vertebrae in the backbone, and a very long tail up to twice that length. The arms and legs are short and broadened a little as paddles. However, the pleurosaurs never became fully aquatic, since the hands and feet could still have been used for slow walking on land, even though they became quite tiny in later forms. It is likely that the pleurosaurs swam by beating their long tails from side to side, and used their arms and legs for steering. The head is unusual, being long and low, and the teeth are like zigzag saw edges, being fused firmly to the bones of the jaws.

The relationships of the pleurosaurs have been difficult to determine. However, a recently discovered specimen in the Early Jurassic seems to be a kind of "missing link" between the tuataras including *Clevosaurus* and the pleurosaurs.

It may be that the tuataras, which were important small lizardlike insect and plant-eaters in the Late Triassic, gave rise to a swimming group as well.

PLIOHIPPUS

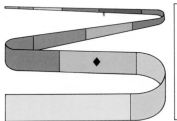

> PLY-oh-HIP-us
? Greater horse
ⓝ J. Leidy (1869)
ⓘ California Texas
♦ Miocene

7ft.

One of the last in the great line of horse evolution was *Pliohippus*, a horse that died out about five million years ago. *Pliohippus* replaced *Merychippus* in North America about 15 million years ago. It was the first horse to have a single toe on each leg. *Merychippus* had only one toe touching the ground, but it still had the two side toes present as small splints on each side of the leg. *Pliohippus* was slightly smaller than a typical modern horse and its teeth were not so deeply rooted. It is an important form since it became widespread in North America and gave rise to one form that invaded South America (which has since died out) and to the true modern horse that spread worldwide, and was tamed by humans later.

Pliohippus

P

POEBROTHERIUM

> PEE-bro-THEE-ree-um
? Grass-eating beast
(n) J. Leidy (1847)
(l) Nebraska South
    Dakota
◆ Oligocene

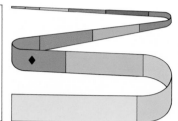

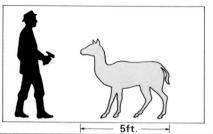

5ft.

The camels today are a small group, containing the one-humped and two-humped camels of Africa and Asia, and the llamas and vicunyas of South America. In the Miocene, from 25 to 5 million years ago, they were a hugely successful group worldwide. One of the oldest camels was *Poebrotherium*, a goat-sized animal with long slender legs and a long neck, as in living forms. The long legs and tiny feet show that this was a fast runner. The feet bear small hooves on the two toes, but these hooves were lost during the evolution of camels and replaced by broad pads, a feature that allows them to walk on soft sand. *Poebrotherium* had long jaws, and the front teeth stuck out forward a little, as in modern camels, which allowed them to bite off plants very close to their roots.

Poebrotherium

PRESBYORNIS

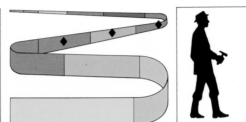

> PREZ-bee-OR-nis
? Old bird
(n) A. Wetmore (1926)
(l) Wyoming Utah South Africa
♦ Cretaceous Eocene

3ft.

The evolution of most modern groups of birds is poorly known. This is because fossils of bird skeletons are not often found, and because most of the modern groups seem to have evolved quite rapidly. One early form that may be related to modern shore birds and waders is *Presbyornis*, which is known from a number of partial skeletons. This bird had long legs with toes that spread out widely and may have been joined by webs of skin. The long legs are typical of runners and the broad feet may have been as much to stop it sinking into soft sand as for swimming. The neck was very long and curved, and the head was large and equipped with a broad beak.

Presbyornis probably ran along the shores of lakes or of the sea, feeding on small water-living shrimps and shellfish. It probably sucked these into its mouth and filtered out the sand and mud before swallowing. Some scientists have argued that *Presbyornis* is a "missing link" between the modern sea birds such as plovers, snipes, and gulls on the one hand, and ducks and geese on the other. The long legs and spreading feet are like those of plovers and snipes, while the head and beak are rather ducklike. The evidence is not good, however, and it may be that *Presbyornis* is not closely related to either group.

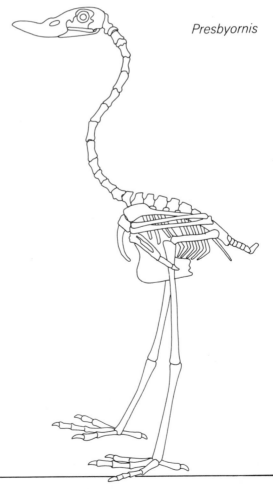

Presbyornis

PROBAINOGNATHUS

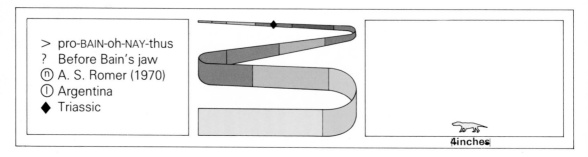

> pro-BAIN-oh-NAY-thus
? Before Bain's jaw
Ⓝ A. S. Romer (1970)
Ⓛ Argentina
◆ Triassic

4inches

The cynodont mammallike reptiles, such as *Cynognathus* and *Thrinaxodon* are generally regarded to be close to the origin of the mammals. One of the most advanced cynodonts is *Probainognathus*, a terrier-sized meat-eater. At first sight, its skeleton and skull seem so similar to those of *Morganucodon*, one of the first mammals, that they might be thought to be the same. However, *Probainognathus* has not quite crossed the dividing line between reptiles and mammals. The hip girdle, shoulder girdle, and rib cage are still reptilelike. The key features are seen in the head region. Mammals have only one bone in the lower jaw, while reptiles have about six, and this is still the case in *Probainognathus*, although five of these bones are tiny so it is still definitely a reptile.

PROCOLOPHON

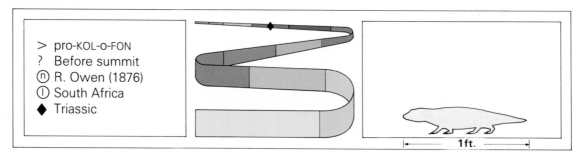

> pro-KOL-o-FON
? Before summit
Ⓝ R. Owen (1876)
Ⓛ South Africa
◆ Triassic

1ft.

Procolophon is a member of a long-lived group of primitive reptiles that arose in the Late Permian and survived to the end of the Triassic some 50 million years later. *Procolophon* was a small plant-eating reptile with an odd triangular shaped skull. The eyes were huge, and there were spinelike outgrowths at the back of the skull. In life, *Procolophon* probably looked like a clumsy lizard, but no living lizard has such a broad head or such heavy limbs. The procolophonids may be related to the pareiasaurs such as *Scutosaurus*.

PROCONSUL

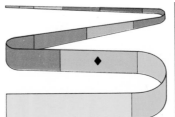

> pro-KON-sul
? Before consul
Ⓝ A. T. Hopwood (1933)
Ⓛ Kenya
◆ Miocene

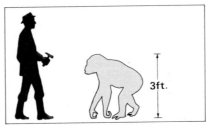

3ft.

The apes may have arisen some 30 million years ago, with a form such as *Aegyptopithecus*, but they first became widespread in the Miocene, some 15 million years later. The first skeleton of *Proconsul* was found over 100 years ago in France, and it was named after the chimpanzee Consul who was then on show in London. *Proconsul* and its close relatives arose in Africa, but they spread over much of the Middle East, southern Europe, and Asia as far as Pakistan and China. *Proconsul* is about the size of a modern rhesus monkey, and it may have run about on the ground, or along stout branches, on all fours. It fed on leaves and fruit.

Proconsul

PROCYNOSUCHUS

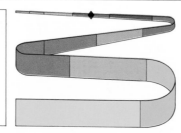

> pro-KINE-O-SOOK-us
? Before dog reptile
ⓝ R. Broom (1937)
ⓛ South Africa
◆ Permian

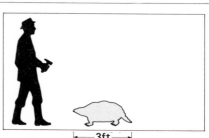

2½ft.

The cynodont reptiles such as *Cynognathus*, *Probainognathus*, and *Thrinaxodon*, were important meat-eaters in the Triassic that gave rise to some plant-eaters like *Diademodon*, and much more importantly, the mammals as well. The first cynodont, *Procynosuchus* arose in the Late Permian. It shows the advanced dog-like face of the later cynodonts, with a large brain, and teeth which are mammallike in some ways. In particular, the cheek teeth were broader than the front teeth and specialized for cutting meat, while the front teeth were used for biting pieces of flesh from the prey animal.

PROGANOCHELYS

> pro-GAN-O-KEEL-is
? Before bright turtle
ⓝ G. Baur (1887)
ⓛ Germany Thailand
◆ Triassic

3ft.

Proganochelys skull

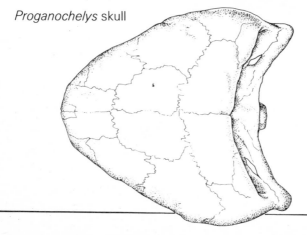

The modern turtles and tortoises seem to be very different from other reptile groups. However, the first turtle, *Proganochelys*, shows some similarities to certain primitive reptiles like *Captorhinus*. *Proganochelys* still had teeth in the roof of its mouth, while modern turtles have lost all trace of teeth.

PROLACERTA

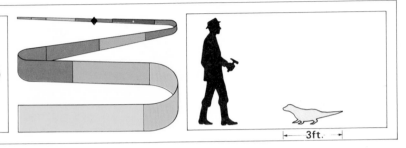

> PRO-la-KER-ta
? Early lizard
ⓝ F. R. Parrington (1935)
Ⓛ South Africa
◆ Triassic

3ft.

For a long time, *Prolacerta* was thought to be one of the first lizards, hence its name. It is certainly larger than most modern lizards, but the long narrow skull and slender body, and especially some features of the bones at the back of the head were thought to be lizard features. The bones of the skull that form the joint with the lower jaw are moveable in

Tanystropheus and some other Triassic forms. These prolacertids seem to be related more to the rhynchosaurs such as *Hyperodapedon* and to the thecodontians, the ancestors of dinosaurs and crocodiles, than to the lizards. Indeed, a close comparison of *Prolacerta* with the first thecodontian, *Proterosuchus*, shows how similar they were.

Prolacerta

modern lizards and snakes, allowing them to open their jaws very wide. It was thought that *Prolacerta* had these specialized lizard features as well.

However, it turns out that this is not the case. *Prolacerta* is closely related to the remarkable

Prolacerta was a fast-running animal which may have reared up on its hind legs sometimes. It probably fed on insects and worms, and it may have used its long neck to get into narrow spaces between tree roots or rocks in order to seek its prey.

PROTEMNODON

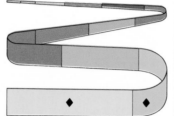

> > pro-TEM-no-don
> ? Early cut tooth
> ⋒ R. Owen (1874)
> ① Australia
> ◆ Pliocene Pleistocene

8ft.

The kangaroos are probably the most "Australian" animals, since they have never been found outside that continent. They move about on their hind legs but do so by taking great leaps instead of running, as we do. It has been calculated that they can move as fast as a race horse, and probably with less effort! Kangaroos today range in size from rabbit-sized wallabies to about human-sized kangaroos. In the past, there were giant kangaroos such as *Protemnodon* that reached a height of 10 feet. *Protemnodon* had a shorter face than modern relatives.

PROTEROSUCHUS

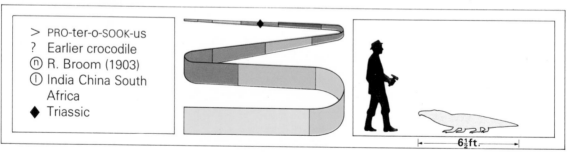

> > PRO-ter-o-SOOK-us
> ? Earlier crocodile
> ⋒ R. Broom (1903)
> ① India China South Africa
> ◆ Triassic

6½ft.

The Triassic period, from 245 to 208 million years ago, saw some major phases in the evolution of land animals. In the Late Triassic, the first turtles, tuataras, dinosaurs, crocodiles, pterosaurs, and mammals appeared, and the mammallike reptiles mostly disappeared. The great changeover started at the beginning of the Triassic with *Proterosuchus*, the first thecodontian, the group that gave rise to crocodiles, pterosaurs, and dinosaurs. *Proterosuchus* was a moderately-sized meat-eating animal, shaped like a small crocodile. It looked a little like its relative *Prolacerta*, but had both crocodile and dinosaur features in the skull and legs. *Proterosuchus* fed on small plant-eaters, and possibly on fish.

PROTOROSAURUS

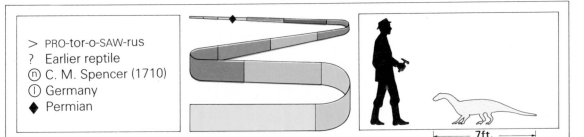

> PRO-tor-o-SAW-rus
? Earlier reptile
ⓝ C. M. Spencer (1710)
Ⓛ Germany
◆ Permian

7ft.

Protorosaurus skeleton (3–6 feet long)

The diapsid reptiles, which today include lizards, snakes, and crocodiles, arose about 310 million years ago with forms such as *Petrolacosaurus*. There is a long gap in their fossil record, right through the 30 million years of the Early Permian when almost nothing is known of the group. Then, in the Late Permian, a variety of forms of diapsid reptiles appeared, including moderate-sized insect-eaters such as *Protorosaurus* and *Youngina*, swimmers such as *Claudiosaurus* and *Hovasaurus*, and gliders such as *Weigeltisaurus*. *Protorosaurus* is known from a few skeletons from central Europe: indeed it was one of the earliest fossil reptiles to be found, the first specimen being collected in about 1750. *Protorosaurus* was about the size of the biggest living lizards, and it was once thought by some scientists to be closely related to the ancestors of lizards. Others thought that it had something to do with the origin of the sea reptiles such as the ichthyosaurs and plesiosaurs. However, it turns out to be very closely related to *Prolacerta* and *Tanystropheus* of the Triassic, and these are related, in turn, to the rhynchosaurs such as *Hyperodapedon* and the thecodontians such as *Proterosuchus*.

Protorosaurus had a long neck which is partly because all the vertebrae of the neck are long, and because it has more of them. The limbs are long and slender and, as in *Prolacerta*, the hind limb is by far the longest, which suggests that *Protorosaurus* was probably able to rear up on its legs at times. It probably fed on insects and small reptiles.

PROTOSUCHUS

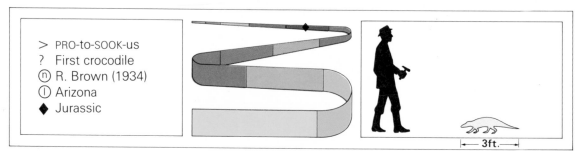

> PRO-to-SOOK-us
? First crocodile
ⓝ R. Brown (1934)
Ⓛ Arizona
◆ Jurassic

3ft.

The first crocodilians first appeared during the Late Triassic, some 225 million years ago, but if you had seen them, you would not have thought they were related to modern crocodiles. They probably looked more like dinosaurs, being small insect-eaters that lived on land and often ran on their hind legs. However, the group took to a life of fish-eating in the water in the Early Jurassic, about 205 million years ago, and they have had some success doing that. The first "true" crocodilian is *Protosuchus*. It still had the long legs of its ancestors, and the hind legs were much longer than the arms, showing that it arose from a two-legged animal. The skull is short, and not yet fully adapted for fish-eating; *Protosuchus* probably fed on small lizard-sized land animals such as the tuataras, surviving mammallike reptiles, and even mammals. *Protosuchus* is covered in an armor made from small square bony plates set in the skin.

Protosuchus

PTERANODON

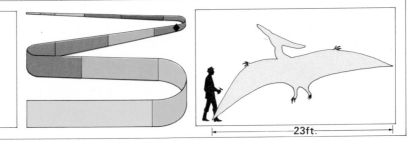

> TER-an-O-don
? Winged toothless
ⓝ O. C. Marsh (1876)
Ⓛ Wyoming
◆ Cretaceous

23ft.

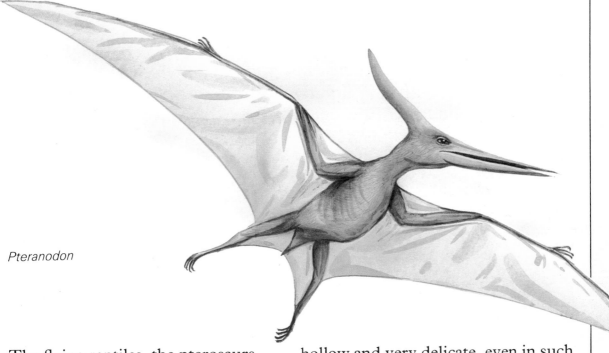

Pteranodon

The flying reptiles, the pterosaurs, ruled the skies during much of the age of the dinosaurs, and one of the most spectacular was *Pteranodon*. This monster animal was much larger than the earliest pterosaurs such as *Dimorphodon*, but smaller than a recently discovered form, *Quetzalcoatlus*. Fossils of *Pteranodon* have been found in a number of parts of the mid-west of North America, and some are quite complete. This is surprising since the bones were hollow and very delicate, even in such a giant as *Pteranodon*. The skeletons show that it had a wing span of 23 feet, much greater than any known bird, living or extinct. *Pteranodon* must have been able to flap its wings since it had all the necessary joints and muscles. Although the wings of *Pteranodon* would have spanned the width of a house, its body probably weighed only about 37 pounds, the weight of a two- or three-year-old child.

PTERODAUSTRO

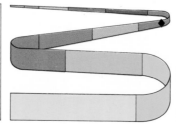

> TER-o-DOW-stro
? Southern wing
(n) J. F. Bonaparte (1970)
(l) Argentina
♦ Cretaceous

4ft.

The most remarkable pterosaur may have been *Pterodaustro*. It was not in any way as large as *Pteranodon* or *Quetzalcoatlus*, but it had the most unusual jaws and teeth. Pterosaurs normally have long pointed jaws, but those of *Pterodaustro* were ten times as long as the rest of the skull. The upper jaw bore a few short teeth, while the lower jaw had as many as two thousand long narrow teeth.

These teeth were probably flexible, like the stiff hairs on a brush, and they were packed closely together. They formed a kind of sieve through which *Pterodaustro* strained small shrimps from the water. It is likely that it flew low over the surface of the waves, trailing its lower jaws just beneath the surface, and raking up mouthfuls of tiny animals.

PTILODUS

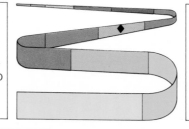

> til-o-dus
? Feather tooth
(n) E. D. Cope (1881)
(l) New Mexico Colorado
♦ Paleocene

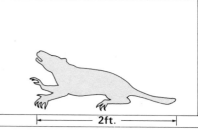

2ft.

The multituberculate mammals, an important extinct group that ranged from the Jurassic to the Oligocene, a time span of 140 million years or so, are known from some good fossils. One of the later forms, *Ptilodus*, shows advances over earlier ones such as *Kamptobaatar* in having more

advanced teeth. It had a long flexible body and grasping hands that show it climbed trees.

Ptilodus

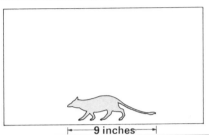

PURGATORIUS

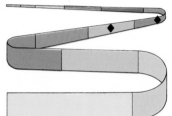

> PUR-ga-TORE-ee-us
? Purified
ⓝ L. Van Valen and R. Sloan (1965)
ⓘ North America
◆ Cretaceous Paleocene

|← 9 inches →|

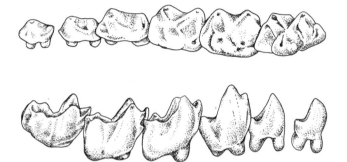

Teeth of *Purgatorius*, an early primate

Humans belong to the mammalian order Primates (which means "first"). This group also includes monkeys, apes, and primitive forms called lemurs, bushbabies, and tarsiers. The Primates were actually one of the first of the modern mammal groups to come to prominence.

A single tooth from the Late Cretaceous of Montana has been identified as *Purgatorius*, and if this is correct, it shows that the first lemurlike animals, our most distant ancestors, were actually present on the earth with the dinosaurs. It is certainly wrong to think of cave dwellers in the days of the dinosaurs, but at least the oldest primates might have seen a dinosaur!

Purgatorius was no match for any dinosaur. It was a small animal that probably looked rather like a squirrel, as is suggested by remains of close relatives from the Paleocene and Eocene, such as *Plesiadapis*. These include nearly complete skulls which show some of the key primate characters such as large eyes (they may have needed large eyes to see at night) and a large brain. The tiny teeth suggest that *Purgatorius* ate a mixed diet of small animals, leaves, and fruit. It may have lived mainly on insects which it caught as it moved quietly among the branches of trees. It was probably safe there from meat-eaters, and relied on its small size and secretive habits for protection.

PYROTHERIUM

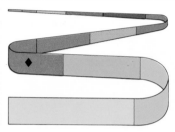

> PY-ro-THEE-ree-um
? Fire beast
ⓝ F. Ameghino (1889)
ⓛ Argentina
◆ Oligocene

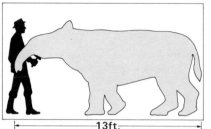

13ft.

Some of the fossil mammals of South America were very odd since they had evolved in isolation from the rest of the world. *Pyrotherium* is a good example, since it probably looked a little like a primitive elephant in some ways, but had many unusual features of its own.

Its name means "fire beast," which refers to the fact that it was found in beds of ancient volcanic ash that had covered over the bones. *Pyrotherium* was a large animal with pillarlike legs to support its weight. It fed on plant food, as is shown by the broad cheek teeth, and it had *six* tusks, not two as in modern elephants, or four as in some fossil forms. These tusks were short and chisellike, and they may have been used for rooting around in the ground for tasty bulbs and roots.

Pyrotherium

QUETZALCOATLUS

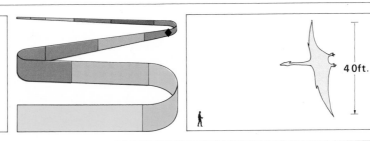

> KWET-zal-KO-at-lus
? Named after an Aztec god
(n) D. A. Lawson (1975)
(l) Texas
◆ Cretaceous

40ft.

For a long time, *Pteranodon* was the largest known flying reptile, or pterosaur, known to science. However, some enormous bones were collected in 1975 in Texas, and they clearly came from a pterosaur that was even larger than *Pteranodon*. The bones included a lower jaw, some neck vertebrae, the upper arm bone, and other parts of the skeleton. The upper arm bone gives some idea of the overall size of the wing, even

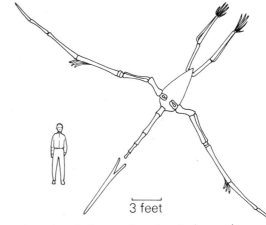

3 feet

Quetzalcoatlus skeleton, showing its huge size compared to that of a man.

though the whole wing has not yet been found. At first, some scientists estimated that *Quetzalcoatlus* had a total wing span of 65 feet or more, the size of a small airplane, but the true figure was probably "only" 36 to 40 feet. This was clearly the largest flying animal that has ever lived. Each wing was as long as a bus, and yet it has been estimated that the body weighed only 110 pounds, the weight of a small man. This is because it takes enormous wings to lift even a light body off the ground; and *Quetzalcoatlus* was nearly five times as large as the largest known bird.

EVOLUTION OF THE REPTILES

The amphibians declined in importance during the Permian period, 286–245 million years ago, because of the rise of the reptiles. Reptiles today include lizards, snakes, crocodiles, and turtles, but they had a much more spectacular past. They owed their success to their ability to lay their eggs on land.

Amphibians have to lay their eggs in the water (think of frog spawn). Reptile eggs, however, have a tough outer shell, as do those of birds, and this stops them from drying out. This allowed the early reptiles, which arose in the Carboniferous, to evolve in many new directions that were closed to the amphibians. They could move away from lake shores and swampy forests into the high lands. The Permian reptiles include the sail-backs, *Dimetrodon* and *Edaphosaurus*, and later mammallike reptiles such as *Moschops*, *Lycaenops*, and *Sauroctonus*.

There were small lizardlike animals such as *Youngina*, monsters such as *Scutosaurus*, and even gliding forms such as *Weigeltisaurus*.

In the Triassic (245–208 million years ago) the mammallike reptiles declined and gave rise to the

Moschops

Youngina

Sauroctonus

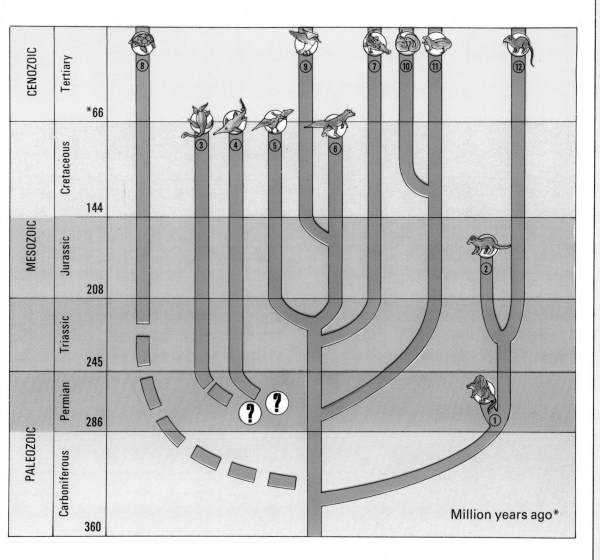

Key to reptilian evolution

1 Sail-backs	7 Crocodiles
2 Mammal-like reptiles	8 Turtles
3 Plesiosaurs	9 Birds
4 Ichthyosaurs	10 Snakes
5 Pterosaurs	11 Lizards
6 Dinosaurs	12 Mammals

Million years ago*

mammals. New groups arose, including the ancestors of crocodiles and dinosaurs, animals like *Proterosuchus*, *Stagonolepis*, and *Ticinosuchus*. New reptile groups emerged near the end of the Triassic: turtles, crocodiles, lizard ancestors, pterosaurs, and dinosaurs. During the age of the dinosaurs (Jurassic and Cretaceous periods, 208–66 million years ago), the pterosaurs flew in the skies above, and the ichthyosaurs and plesiosaurs swam in the seas below. All of these died out at the start of the age of the mammals.

RAMAPITHECUS

> ram-a-PITH-eh-kus
? Rama ape
Ⓝ G. E. Pilgrim (1910)
Ⓛ Turkey India Pakistan
  Kenya
◆ Miocene Pliocene

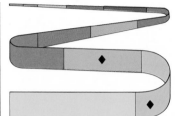

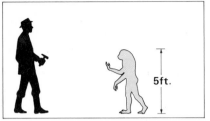

5ft.

The early stages of the evolution of apes and humans all took place in Africa. The oldest ape, *Aegyptopithecus*, dates from about 30 million years ago, and several lines of apes arose in the Miocene, including *Proconsul* and *Ramapithecus*. Indeed, if you had returned to eastern Africa about 10 or 15 million years ago, you would have found dozens of ape species living in the woodlands and open savannahs. The oldest specimens of *Ramapithecus* come from Africa, but it seems that this ape soon spread

Ramapithecus skull. This primate was closely related to the early homonids.

to many parts of the world, including southern Europe, the Middle East, India, southern Asia, and China. This great spread of the early apes could only happen in the Middle Miocene, some 13 million years ago, since Africa had been an island until then. At that time, a narrow strip of land formed between Egypt and Arabia, and animals could move in and out of Africa. Until the 1980s, *Ramapithecus* was known only from teeth and jaws.

These seemed to be "missing links" between the teeth and jaws of modern apes and modern humans, and to fall on the human line. Then, in 1983, some much more complete specimens were found in India, and these included a skull. This shows a massive lower jaw, large teeth, a long apelike snout, and a relatively small braincase. *Ramapithecus* clearly was not an early human form, but seemed now to fall near the beginning of the line leading to the orangutans, apes that now live in Southeast Asia. The "human" features of the teeth must be seen as parallel developments. This shows the importance of finding complete fossils!

RHAMPHORHYNCHUS

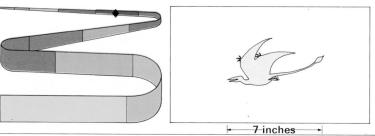

> RAM-for-INK-us
? Curving snout
ⓝ H. von Meyer (1847)
ⓛ Tanzania Bavaria
◆ Jurassic

7 inches

Most of the early pterosaurs, such as *Dimorphodon* and *Rhamphorhynchus*, belong to a primitive group called the rhamphorhynchoids. They have a long tail, and do not have all of the specializations of the backbone and legs of the later pterodactyloids. Also, they never reached the large size of later forms like *Pteranodon* and

Rhamphorhynchus

Quetzalcoatlus. Rhamphorhynchus reached seagull size and had long narrow wings made from skin stretched over a very long fourth finger of the hand.

Many of the fossils are very well preserved, being found in the same beds as *Archaeopteryx*, and they show that *Rhamphorhynchus* was covered with hair. They also show the shape of the wing, the presence of a loose throat pouch (to hold fish, as in a pelican?), and a square vane at the end of the long tail. The tail was used for steering.

SAMOTHERIUM

> SAME-o-THEE-ree-um
?
ⓝ C. I. Forsyth-Major (1888)
ⓘ Turkey Europe Africa
◆ Miocene Pliocene

|—— 10ft. ——|

The giraffes have a patchy fossil record. They are closely related to the deer and cattle, and certain fossils from the Early Miocene, 25 to 15 million years ago, of Europe and Africa, could belong to any of these three groups. One of the first definite giraffes is *Samotherium*. It had a long skull with projecting teeth at the front of its lower jaw for cropping leaves, and broad cheek teeth behind for grinding its food. It is known to be a giraffe since it had a pair of short bony "horns" sticking up above the eyes. In life, these would have been covered by skin, as in modern giraffes. Giraffe "horns" are not so obvious as those of cattle and deer, but they are always present, even if small.

SCUTOSAURUS

> SKOOT-o-SAW-rus
? Armored reptile
ⓝ A. Hartmann-Weinberg (1930)
ⓘ Russia
◆ Permian

|—— 8ft. ——|

The most foolish reptiles of all time may have been the pareiasaurs of the Late Permian. Typical forms, like *Scutosaurus*, have a barrellike body and massive legs. The head is tiny in comparison (compare these proportions with any other reptile of its day) which suggests a tiny brain.

The teeth show that *Scutosaurus* was a plant-eater, and the skull is armored with spines and knobs.

SEBECUS

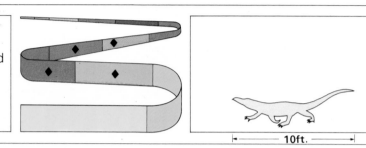

> SEB-e-kus
? Egyptian crocodile god
ⓝ G. G. Simpson (1937)
ⓛ South Africa
◆ Paleocene Miocene

|← 10ft. →|

Crocodiles today are a fairly minor group of reptiles, with only 20 or so species. However, in the past they have included a great variety of forms that achieved some importance in the sea, such as *Geosaurus* and *Teleosaurus*, others that lived on land and in the sea, like the modern forms, and some that hunted mainly on land, such as *Protosuchus* and *Sebecus*. The remains of *Sebecus* and its relatives have been found over much of South America and one from the first half of the age of mammals. Possible relatives are represented by remains from Europe and North Africa. However, the sebecids had their heyday in South America.

Sebecus has a high long-snouted skull. All of the bones of the skull are covered with a sculpture of pits and grooves, as is typical of crocodiles. The heavy lower jaw extends well behind the back of the skull and it clearly carried powerful muscles. The key feature of the sebecids lies in the teeth which are flat and daggerlike, instead of round in cross section, as in other crocodiles. In addition, the teeth of *Sebecus* have zigzag sawlike

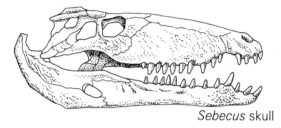

Sebecus skull

edges which were used to cut meat, just like a steak knife. Indeed, the teeth of *Sebecus* look exactly like those of a meat-eating dinosaur such as *Tyrannosaurus*, instead of like those of a crocodile. In the past, many scientists found odd sebecid teeth and announced that they had discovered dinosaurs in Tertiary rocks, long after they were supposed to have died out!

The sebecids were large, and probably fed on many of the South American plant-eating mammals until about 15 million years ago when they were replaced by large meat-eating birds such as *Phorusrhacos*. At the same time, various mammals such as *Andrewsarchus*, *Hyaenodon*, *Mesonyx*, *Oxyaena*, and the first cats and dogs, fed on the plant-eating mammals in other parts of the world. It is a remarkable fact that in South America, these roles were first taken by crocodiles, and then by birds!

SEYMOURIA

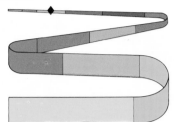

> see-MOOR-ee-a
? For Dr. Seymour
ⓝ F. Broili (1904)
ⓘ Oklahoma Texas Utah
  New Mexico
◆ Permian

The first specimens of *Seymouria* were quickly recognized to be a kind of "missing link" between the amphibians and the reptiles. It is reptilelike in having a high skull and fairly long legs. It was found in rocks that were laid down in dry conditions, so it presumably spent most of its time away from water. In addition, a fossil egg was reported that might have been laid by *Seymouria*. If the specimen is an egg, and that is not certain, it must have been laid by a reptile since it has a hard shell; amphibian eggs (like frog spawn) have no shell.

However, it is now known that the reptiles arose at least 50 million years, and possibly 90 million, before *Seymouria* emerged, so it cannot be an ancestor. It is closely related to *Diadectes* and *Limnoscelis*. *Seymouria* was a fairly active meat-eater, and it may have fed on other amphibians such as *Diplocaulus* or on small reptiles like *Captorhinus*.

Seymouria

SINCLAIRELLA

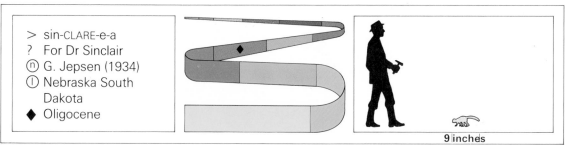

> sin-CLARE-e-a
? For Dr Sinclair
Ⓝ G. Jepsen (1934)
Ⓛ Nebraska South Dakota
◆ Oligocene

9 inches

An odd little group of animals called apatemyids lived in the early years of the age of mammals. Typical examples, such as *Sinclairella*, probably looked a little like shrews, but their teeth were most peculiar. They had broad cheek teeth that were presumably used for crushing tough food, and extremely long front teeth in the upper and lower jaws that curved forward like long tusks. In some ways, these long front teeth are like those of rodents such as rats and mice, since they appear to have grown continuously and to have sharpened themselves against each other. Unfortunately, no one has found any of the skeleton of the apatemyids, so it is hard to guess how they lived. It is even hard to figure out what they ate.

SINOCONODON

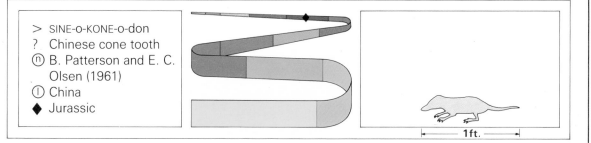

> SINE-o-KONE-o-don
? Chinese cone tooth
Ⓝ B. Patterson and E. C. Olsen (1961)
Ⓛ China
◆ Jurassic

1 ft.

One of the most primitive mammals, *Sinoconodon*, is known only from partial skull remains. The skull is small, and in many ways still seems to be like a cynodont mammallike reptile such as *Cynognathus* or *Probainognathus*. The lower jaw shows that it is a mammal, however. Although *Sinoconodon* lived at the same time as *Morganucodon*, it seems that both forms belong to different branches of mammal evolution.

Sinoconodon skull (2 inches long)

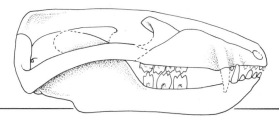

SIVATHERIUM

> SEE-va-THEE-ree-um
? Siva beast
ⓝ H. Falconer and P. Cautley (1836)
① East Asia Africa
◆ Pliocene Pleistocene

8ft.

It would be easy to assume that fossil giraffes all look like the modern forms, but possibly with shorter necks. This is true of many, such as *Samotherium*. However, there have been some bizarre side branches of giraffe evolution during their short history. *Sivatherium* is an Indian form that probably looked more like a giant moose than a giraffe. It had a short neck and a massive head about 28 inches long. There was a pair of short "horns" covered in skin over the eyes, a characteristic of giraffes. Behind these were two more horns that spread out into broad curving plates with a number of points. These great "antlers" were fully developed only in the males, and they were probably used in fighting for mates.

SMILODECTES

> SMILE-o-DEK-teez
? Chisel biter
ⓝ O. C. Marsh (1871)
① Wyoming
◆ Eocene

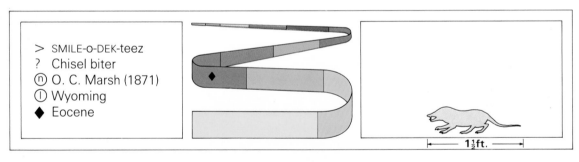

1½ft.

The Primates, which today include monkeys, apes, and humans, arose over 67 million years ago, with the lemurlike *Purgatorius*. Early primates like this, and the later *Plesiadapis*, probably looked rather like squirrels, although they had better eyesight and larger brains.

Several groups of "pre-monkeys" arose in these early days, and one of the more advanced were the adapids such as *Smilodectes*. This animal appears to be related to the modern lemurs of Madagascar. It had a long tail and strong grasping hands and feet that allowed it to climb trees with agility. *Smilodectes* also showed advanced features in its skull. The braincase and eyes were large, and the snout short.

SMILODON

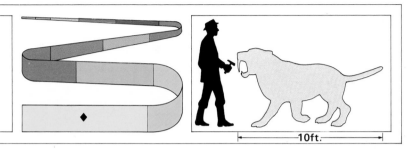

> SMILE-o-don
? Chisel tooth
Ⓝ J Leidy (1868)
Ⓛ Argentina
◆ Pleistocene

10ft.

The cat family has included a great variety of meat-eating types that no longer exist. The most spectacular were the saber-toothed cats such as *Smilodon* which had massive fangs about 6 inches long. They could drop their lower jaws to a right angle in order to clear these great stabbing teeth, and then use them to pierce the thick hides of even the largest plant-eaters. There were massive muscles at the back of the neck which allowed *Smilodon* to hammer these great teeth into its prey. It was once thought that the saber-toothed cats simply stabbed through the skin and let their victims bleed. However, the tips of the teeth are not generally very sharp, and the force needed to drive them straight into a thick-skinned plant-eater would have been very great. New studies suggest that *Smilodon* took a fold of skin in its mouth and bit a chunk out, which would have made its victim bleed to death all the faster.

Smilodon

STAGONOLEPIS

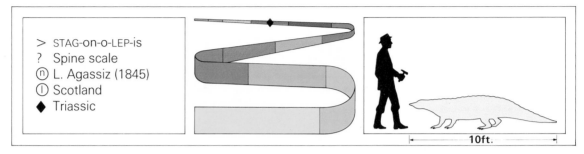

> STAG-on-o-LEP-is
? Spine scale
(n) L. Agassiz (1845)
(l) Scotland
◆ Triassic

10ft.

Stagonolepis belongs to an unusual group of thecodontians that ate plants. Most of the thecodontians, such as *Erythrosuchus*, *Lagosuchus*, *Proterosuchus*, and *Ticinosuchus* were meat-eaters, and they include the ancestors of the dinosaurs and of the crocodiles. *Stagonolepis* lies on the line to crocodiles, and it is closely related to *Ticinosuchus*. *Stagonolepis* looks roughly crocodilian; it has a long low body, with a deep powerful tail and short legs. It was also covered in broad sheets of armor that ran right along the back from the neck to the tip of the tail, as well as under the belly and under the tail. The armor was made from rectangles of bone shaped like playing cards that were formed in the skin. These bony plates overlapped like the slates on a roof, and they were held together by bony pegs. This bony armor may have been necessary to prevent attacks by the large and active meat-eaters of the time, such as *Ornithosuchus* and *Ticinosuchus*.

It is clear that *Stagonolepis* was a harmless plant-eater when you look at its head. The jaws are short and lined with peglike teeth. There is also a strange "snub" nose. *Stagonolepis* probably dug for tasty roots and bulbs with the upturned tip of its snout. The relatives of *Stagonolepis* lived in most parts of the world, and gave way to large plant-eating dinosaurs.

STYLINODON

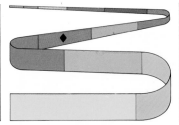

> sty-LIN-o-don
? Pillar tooth
(n) O. C. Marsh (1847)
(l) Wyoming Utah Asia
♦ Eocene

One of the first large plant-eating mammals was *Stylinodon*, possibly distantly related to *Pantolambda*. *Stylinodon* reached the size of a bear, and it had advanced adaptations for dealing with tough plant food. The jaws were massive and there were two kinds of teeth. The front teeth were long and chisellike, just right for cutting through wood or fibrous plants. The cheek teeth were broad, and they continued to grow throughout its life, as in modern plant-eaters. This allowed the cheek teeth to wear down. (Our teeth do not grow continuously.)

Stylinodon had strong, deep claws on its hands and feet, which were probably used for digging up roots.

SYNTHETOCERAS

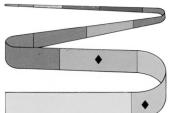

> SIN-thet-o-SER-as
? Compound skull
(n) R. A. Stirton (1932)
(l) Texas
♦ Miocene Pliocene

The protoceratids were an odd group of horned animals, possibly related to the camels, that lived in North America for 55 million years. *Synthetoceras* was a large long-legged animal that probably looked a little like a deer. The males had a long Y-shaped horn like a catapult on the tip of the snout, while females and young animals did not. It may have been used by males in fighting for females, just as deer do today. In fighting, this long horn must have been used in upward stabs. Other protoceratids had long horns behind the ears, V-shaped nose horns, or two or three pairs of short horns over the nose, eyes, and ears.

TANYSTROPHEUS

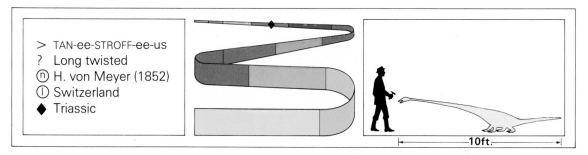

> TAN-ee-STROFF-ee-us
? Long twisted
ⓝ H. von Meyer (1852)
① Switzerland
◆ Triassic

The oddest-looking fossil reptile must be *Tanystropheus*. It had an enormously long neck, more than twice the length of its body and tail together, and yet there were only 12 vertebrae in the neck, each being 6 inches long or more. Other long-necked reptiles, such as the plesiosaur *Elasmosaurus*, had dozens of neck vertebrae so that it could be bent around a great deal. *Tanystropheus* could have bent its neck, but only in a broad curve. The young had short necks like *Protorosaurus*, but the neck then shot out in length as *Tanystropheus* grew up. The teeth also changed during growth. Young *Tanystropheus* had small teeth with several points, probably used for capturing insects, while the adults had larger pointed teeth for fish-eating.

TELEOSAURUS

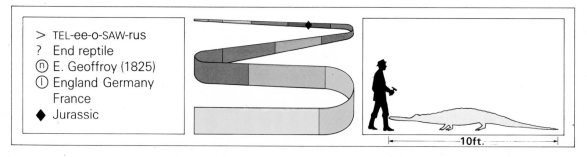

> TEL-ee-o-SAW-rus
? End reptile
ⓝ E. Geoffroy (1825)
① England Germany
　France
◆ Jurassic

During the Jurassic, two groups of crocodiles became adapted to a life in the sea, the teleosaurs such as *Teleosaurus*, and the geosaurs.

　Teleosaurus was a slender animal with a long tail which was used in swimming. The hands and feet are not modified to paddles like those of the later *Geosaurus*, so that *Teleosaurus* probably walked on land as well as swimming. It had a very long, narrow snout.

TERATORNIS

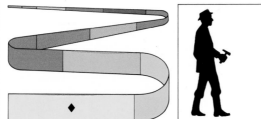

> TER-a-TORN-is
? Monster bird
ⓝ L. H. Miller
ⓛ Argentina California
   Nevada Florida
◆ Pleistocene

5ft.

Teratornis

The largest birds of all time were the teratorns, great vultures that lived in the Americas from 10 million years until a few thousand years ago. The largest teratorn had a wing span of over 23 feet, about the same as *Pteranodon*, but much smaller than *Quetzalcoatlus*, the largest pterosaur.

Teratornis itself was rather smaller, but still a giant, which fed on the carcases of mammoths, rhinoceroses and other plant-eaters that had been killed by saber-toothed cats such as *Smilodon*. Some of the best specimens of *Teratornis* come from the famous La Brea tar pits in California, where large plant-eating mammals were trapped in sticky pools of tar. *Teratornis* came down to feed, and was then trapped itself.

TERRESTRISUCHUS

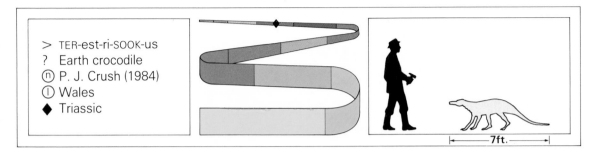

> TER-est-ri-SOOK-us
? Earth crocodile
ⓝ P. J. Crush (1984)
ⓛ Wales
◆ Triassic

7ft.

The first crocodilelike animals were, surprisingly, lightly built insect-eaters such as *Terrestrisuchus*. This is clearly a close ancestor of the true crocodiles since it has special features of the wrist, hip girdle, and skull that only they have. It is a small slender animal that lived on land and may even have run on its hind legs. Only in the Early Jurassic, did crocodiles like *Protosuchus* move toward a life in the water.

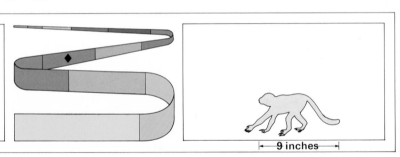

Terrestrisuchus

TETONIUS

> tet-OWN-ee-us
? From Grand Teton
ⓝ W. D. Matthew (1915)
ⓛ North America
◆ Eocene

9 inches

The tarsier is an unusual living primate, a small animal with huge eyes which hunts insects at night in the forests of Southeast Asia. It is a "pre-monkey" form, but shows advanced features in its large brain and enormous eyes. *Tetonius* was a fossil tarsierlike animal which may have looked rather similar. The snout was short and the large eyes both faced forward instead of sideways, as in most other mammals. This is one of the key primate features which we have. When the eyes are close together and face forward, it is possible to see in three dimensions. The field of view of each eye overlaps, which gives "depth" to the scene. Most mammals see a separate scene with each eye and to them everything must look "flat" and distances become very difficult to judge.

THEOSODON

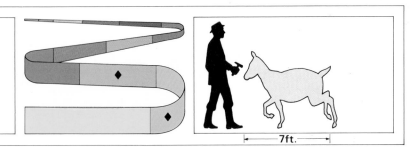

> THEE-o-SO-don
? God tooth
ⓝ F. Ameghino (1887)
① Argentina
◆ Oligocene Miocene

7ft.

The litopterns were an important group of South American mammals that includes horselike forms such as *Thoatherium*, and others that looked a little like camels, such as *Macrauchenia* and *Theosodon*.

The first litopterns probably arose from condylarths like *Phenacodus*, and they include some tiny long-legged forms no larger than rabbits. The litopterns soon became larger and came to mimic camels and horses, since those groups had not entered South America, which was an island at the time. *Theosodon* had a long neck which allowed it to feed on leaves from fairly tall bushes and trees, and it had long legs which allowed it to run fast to escape attacks from the giant meat-eating birds like *Phorusrhacos*.

Tetonius

155

THOATHERIUM

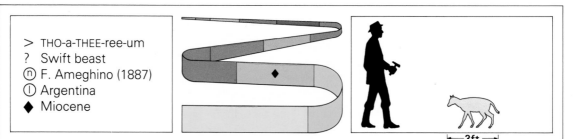

> THO-a-THEE-ree-um
? Swift beast
(n) F. Ameghino (1887)
(l) Argentina
◆ Miocene

├─3ft.─┤

One of the most spectacular examples of "parallel evolution," the evolution of similar animals from different ancestors, is between the South American litopterns and the horses.

While true horses such as *Merychippus* and *Pliohippus* were becoming like the modern horse in North America, *Thoatherium* went one better in many respects. Like those true horses, *Thoatherium* had a single hoof on each leg, but there is no trace at all of the old side toes which were still present in *Merychippus*. *Thoatherium* had the legs, body and head of a horse. So how do we know that it is not a horse, but a relative of *Macrauchenia* and *Theosodon*? Firstly, some features of the upper parts of the leg are quite unlike those of horses, and the teeth are very different. They are essentially the same as in the other South American plant-eaters.

Thoatherium

THRINAXODON

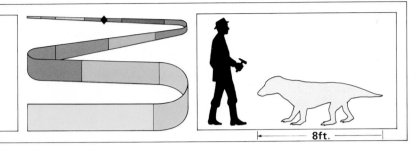

> THRIN-ax-O-don
? Trident tooth
ⓝ H. G. Seeley (1894)
① South Africa
   Antarctica
◆ Triassic

8ft.

Thrinaxodon

Thrinaxodon is a cynodont mammallike reptile, which lies between *Procynosuchus* and *Probainognathus* and the mammals. The skeleton is long and low, and the tail is short. *Thrinaxodon* had a rather primitive posture about midway between the fully sprawling limbs of lizards and sail-backed reptiles such as *Dimetrodon*, and the fully upright position of mammals in which the legs are tucked right beneath the body. In *Thrinaxodon*, the legs still stuck out a little sideways. The rib cage is unusual since the ribs are broad and they overlap, forming a closed barrellike structure. This probably held the body rigid, and would have prevented *Thrinaxodon* from bending much from side to side.

If the body of *Thrinaxodon* is rather primitive, its skull shows many mammallike characters. The head probably looked rather doglike. The long high snout shows that *Thrinaxodon* had a good sense of smell for seeking its prey. The teeth are divided into front nippers, long fangs and cutting cheek teeth with several points like those of *Cynognathus*.

THYLACOLEO

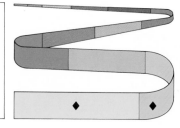

> THY-la-KOLE-ee-o
? Pouched lion
ⓝ R. Owen (1859)
ⓘ Australia
◆ Pliocene Pleistocene

|← 4ft. →|

The major groups of mammals in Australia have always been marsupials, and some of these evolved to look very like the placental mammals of other continents. *Thylacoleo*, the marsupial "lion," was the largest Australian meat-eater, reaching the size of a leopard.

In life, it probably looked rather like a lion, with its short broad head, and powerful limbs. However, the teeth of *Thylacoleo* are very different from those of a lion. The stabbing teeth at the front are modified from the incisors, the front nipping teeth, rather than from the canines. Also, the cheek teeth are like long blades instead of separate points.

THYLACOSMILUS

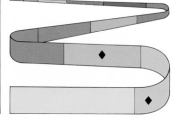

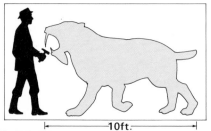

> THY-lak-o-Smile-us
? Pouched chisel
ⓝ E. S. Riggs (1933)
ⓘ Argentina
◆ Miocene Pliocene

|← 10ft. →|

The South American marsupials were good at mimicking placental mammals. *Thylacosmilus*, the saber-toothed South American meat-eater, probably looked just like *Smilodon*. It had long stabbing teeth which were used to pierce the thick skin of plant-eaters. However, it is not related to the true cats at all, but to other South American meat-eaters like *Borhyaena*.

Thylacosmilus

TICINOSUCHUS

> TIK-in-o-SOOK-us
? Tessin crocodile
ⓝ B. Krebs (1963)
ⓘ Switzerland
◆ Triassic

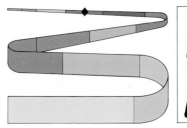

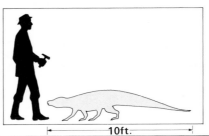

10ft.

One of the most successful groups of thecodontians were the rauisuchids, a group that lies fairly close to the origin of the crocodiles. The rauisuchids were the main meat-eaters in all parts of the world for much of the Triassic. Early forms like *Ticinosuchus* fed on plant-eating mammallike reptiles such as *Diademodon* and *Kannemeyeria*, but good skeletons but unfortunately the skull is incomplete in these. *Ticinosuchus* had a slender body, long limbs that probably allowed it to run fast, and a long tail. Like crocodiles and its other relatives such as *Stagonolepis*, *Ticinosuchus* has some armor plates running down the middle of its back. The neck is long, and the skull deep and rather

Ticinosuchus

later rauisuchids probably preyed on dinosaurs. The group finally disappeared at the end of the Triassic at a time when many other reptile groups were wiped out, possibly by a major change in the environment.

Ticinosuchus is known from a few dinosaurlike. This confused a number of scientists, who thought that the rauisuchids were ancestral to the dinosaurs. Some even mis-identified rauisuchid teeth and jaws as belonging to early dinosaurs because they are so similar.

T

TOXODON

> TOX-o-don
? Bow tooth
ⓝ R. Owen (1840)
① Argentina
◆ Pliocene Pleistocene

9ft.

When Charles Darwin visited South America in the 1830s, he found fossil remains of several unusual animals, including *Macrauchenia* and *Toxodon*. Darwin noted how *Toxodon* seemed to share some characteristics with the rodents (its long front teeth) and others with the elephants (its large size). He wrote: "How wonderfully are the different orders blended together in different points of the structure of the toxodon!" We now know that *Toxodon*, like the other South American plant-eaters, was not closely related to any of the well-known mammal groups that evolved in other parts of the world. The toxodonts are related to forms like *Notostylops* and they arose 50 million years ago. *Toxodon* was one of the last, and the largest. Its head was very rhinoceroslike, and it is likely that *Toxodon* fed on grasses which it cropped with its long front teeth and crushed with its cheek teeth. It was a massive, slow-moving animal.

Toxodon

TRIADOBATRACHUS

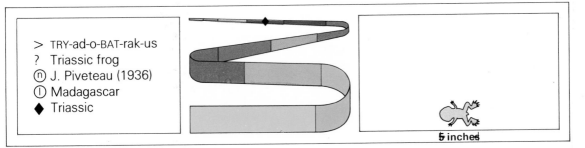

> TRY-ad-o-BAT-rak-us
? Triassic frog
ⓝ J. Piveteau (1936)
Ⓘ Madagascar
◆ Triassic

5 inches

The origin of modern frogs is rather mysterious. The problem is that even the oldest frogs, which date from 200 million years ago in the Early Jurassic, look quite like modern frogs. They have long hind legs, short arms, a short back, no ribs and a broad rounded head.

Triadobatrachus may be a "missing link" between the ancestors of frogs and the true frogs. It still has a long back and short ribs, and the legs are not much longer than the arms. It has the head of a frog and the body of something like *Branchiosaurus* or a small version of *Eryops*.

Triadobatrachus probably moved about by jumping.

TRICONODON

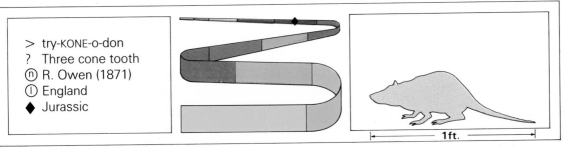

> try-KONE-o-don
? Three cone tooth
ⓝ R. Owen (1871)
Ⓘ England
◆ Jurassic

1 ft.

The evolution of mammals in the Jurassic is a mystery since most of the fossils are very poor, and there is a long gap after forms like *Morganucodon* and before advanced animals like *Deltatheridium* or *Zalambdalestes*. *Triconodon*, known only from a lower jaw and other scrappy material, was a small insect-

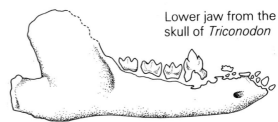

Lower jaw from the skull of *Triconodon*

eater that may lie on a side branch from the main line of mammal evolution.

TRILOPHOSAURUS

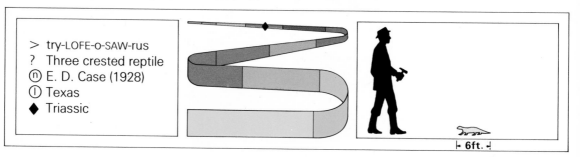

> try-LOFE-o-SAW-rus
? Three crested reptile
ⓝ E. D. Case (1928)
① Texas
◆ Triassic

6ft.

Several unusual groups of reptiles existed for a short time in the Triassic period before dying out. *Trilophosaurus*, a relative of *Hyperodapedon* and of *Prolacerta*, has a very strange skull. It is closed in by solid bone in the cheek region and has a bony beak at the front, almost like a turtle. However, the body was quite lightly built, which suggests an active lifestyle, and it has broad cheek teeth for grinding tough plant food.

Trilophosaurus skeleton
(6 feet long)

TROGOSUS

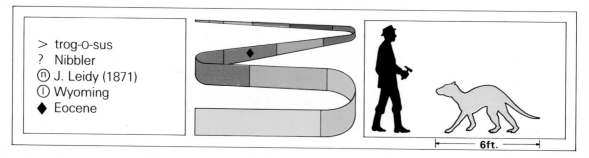

> trog-O-sus
? Nibbler
ⓝ J. Leidy (1871)
① Wyoming
◆ Eocene

6ft.

Trogosus was an unusual bear-sized plant-eater that probably fed on roots and leaves. It is a tillodont, a group of animals that lived for a short time in the Paleocene and Eocene of North America, Europe, and eastern Asia. The tillodonts are known only from skulls, so their lifestyle is still largely a mystery. They had long rodentlike gnawing front teeth and broad grinding cheek teeth. The jaws are heavy and powerful. The tillodonts may be related to the pantodonts like *Pantolambda* and the taeniodonts like *Stylinodon*, but this is uncertain until more complete specimens are found.

UINTATHERIUM

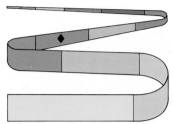

- > oo-IN-ta-THEE-ree-um
- ? Uinta mammal
- ⓝ J. Leidy (1872)
- ① Utah
- ◆ Eocene

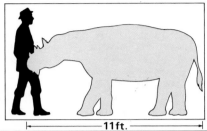

11ft.

The uintatheres, which include *Dinoceras* and *Uintatherium*, were the first large plant-eaters. They probably looked a little like rhinoceroses, but their horns were different, consisting of three pairs of short knobs over the snout, eyes, and ears. The uintatheres lived from the Late Paleocene to the Late Eocene in North America and China, and the brontotheres took over from them as large plant-eaters.

Uintatherium

VULPAVUS

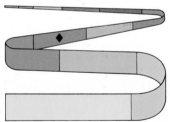

- > vulp-AV-us
- ? Wolf uncle
- ⓝ O. C. Marsh (1871)
- ① North America
- ◆ Eocene

2½ft.

The first advanced meat-eating mammals were the miacids such as *Vulpavus* which arose in the Early Eocene, 53 million years ago. The miacids had short limbs, a long body, and large feet with grasping claws that allowed them to climb trees. *Vulpavus* had a long skull with sharp little teeth, and it probably hunted small insect-eating mammals, birds and lizards, in the trees. In life, it would have looked rather like a pine marten. The miacids are a large group of small meat-eaters from the Eocene of Europe and North America, and it is thought they may have given rise to most of the modern groups, the cats, dogs, and bears.

WEIGELTISAURUS

> wy-GELT-ih-SAW-rus
? Weigelt's reptile
ⓝ O. Kuhn (1939)
ⓛ England Germany
   Madagascar
♦ Permian

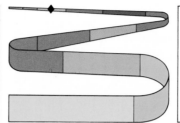

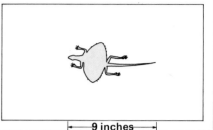

9 inches

Weigeltisaurus

The first reptiles to take to the air were the weigeltisaurs. *Weigeltisaurus* was interpreted as a flying lizard at first, something like the modern *Draco*, a lizard that sails many tens of yards between the tree tops in search of insects to eat. It turns out that *Weigeltisaurus* is a primitive diapsid reptile, not a lizard, and part of a diversification of these small animals in the Late Permian, which included such forms as *Claudiosaurus*, *Hovasaurus*, *Protorosaurus*, and *Youngina*. Fortunately, the specimens of *Weigeltisaurus* are all well preserved, and they show the delicate details of this remarkable little animal. The ribs down each side of the body are very long in the middle of the back, and they become shorter toward the front and towards the back. This gives a symmetrical flat wing shape which was presumably covered with skin in life.

Weigeltisaurus could glide from tree to tree, but it could not flap its "wings" like a bird or bat.

YOUNGINA

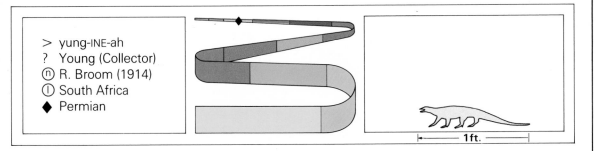

> yung-INE-ah
? Young (Collector)
Ⓝ R. Broom (1914)
Ⓛ South Africa
◆ Permian

1ft.

Youngina was a small lizardlike animal. For some time, it was thought to be the ancestor of the lizards and of the thecodontians, crocodiles and dinosaurs. More recent studies have turned up a variety of relatives of *Youngina* in the Late Permian of Africa and Madagascar, forms such as *Hovasaurus*, and these all seem to be distantly related to the lizards and tuataras.

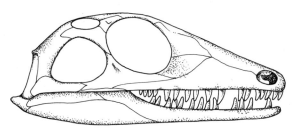

Side view of *Youngina* skull

Youngina has a small lightweight skull very like its distant ancestor *Petrolacosaurus*. The teeth are sharp, but fairly broad, which suggests that it may have had a diet of hard-skinned insects, or even snails. The teeth would have to be broad in this case in order to prevent them from breaking when it cracked open one of these small animals. The back part of the skull is quite high which suggests the presence of strong jaw muscles to operate the jaws.

The skeleton of *Youngina* is not completely known, but it shows a number of lizardlike features. For example, the neck is short, whereas the ancestors of the thecodontians such as *Protorosaurus* and *Prolacerta*

have long necks. There is also a broad bony breast bone which joins the ribs together in the chest region. This is a special feature of lizards. The hands and feet are large and the fingers and toes long and thin, another feature seen in modern lizards.

Youngina and its relatives seem to have died out at the end of the Permian period, a time of major changeover among the animals on land; the pareiasaurs such as *Scutosaurus* disappeared, as did many of the mammallike reptiles.

ZALAMBDALESTES

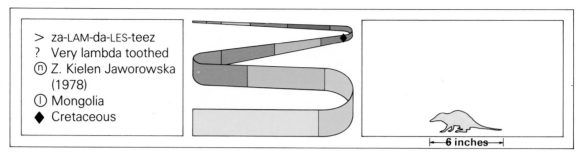

> za-LAM-da-LES-teez
? Very lambda toothed
ⓝ Z. Kielen Jaworowska (1978)
ⓘ Mongolia
◆ Cretaceous

|← 6 inches →|

One of the best known early mammals that lived side by side with the last dinosaurs is *Zalambdalestes* from Mongolia. Beautifully preserved skeletons of this little shrewlike animal have been found in the same deposits as *Kennalestes*, but nearly every part of the body of *Zalambdalestes* is known, except the tail, the ribs, and the front of the snout. *Zalambdalestes* had a long snout lined with small sharp insect-eating teeth. It probably had a good sense of smell which would have allowed it to sniff out its prey. The skeleton shows a number of features seen in modern jumping mammals, like rabbits and kangaroo rats; the hind leg is long and slender in order to provide a strong kick off for the jump, while the arms and backbone are strong in order to take up the sudden force of landing.

Zalambdalestes is one of the earliest placental mammals, and it may be close to the origin of groups such as the insectivores, primates, and bats.

Zalambdalestes

ZYGORHIZA

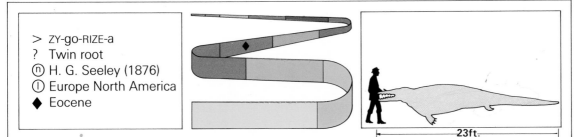

> ZY-go-RIZE-a
? Twin root
(n) H. G. Seeley (1876)
(l) Europe North America
◆ Eocene

23ft.

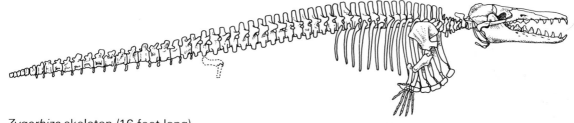

Zygorhiza skeleton (16 feet long)

The whales and dolphins arose from land-living animals in the Late Paleocene or Early Eocene, with forms like *Pakicetus* as a possible "missing link." By Late Eocene times, the whale group had diversified and included giant whales such as *Basilosaurus*, as well as smaller forms such as *Zygorhiza* which probably looked rather like a large porpoise.

Zygorhiza had a long-snouted skull with broad pointed teeth spaced out along the jaws. It is still possible to distinguish the simple pointed peg-like teeth at the front of the jaws from the broader triangular-shaped cheek teeth behind. This is a primitive feature which harks back to the origin of the whales from meat-eating land animals. Modern toothed whales,

such as porpoises and dolphins, have many identical teeth in their jaws with no change in shape from front to back. *Zygorhiza* probably hunted fish in the shallow seas around the shores of North America and Europe.

The skeleton of *Zygorhiza* shows a powerful tail, a deep rib cage, a short neck, and short paddlelike arms. The legs have not been found; they were probably present as reduced splints of bone as in *Basilosaurus* and modern whales. It is likely that *Zygorhiza* had a broad flat tail fin attached to the end of its backbone, as in modern forms.

The arms would have been used for steering. It may be that *Zygorhiza* lies close to the origin of all modern types of whales and dolphins.

MUSEUM GUIDE

The museums listed here are those that have the most outstanding collections of the prehistoric animals shown in this book.

AFRICA
Kenya National Museum, Nairobi, Kenya.
Museum of Earth Sciences, Rabat, Morocco.
National Museum, Niamey, Niger.
South African Museum, Capetown, South Africa.

NORTH AND SOUTH AMERICA
American Museum of Natural History, New York, New York.
Carnegie Museum of Natural History, Pittsburgh, Pennsylvania.
Field Museum of Natural History, Chicago, Illinois
Los Angeles County Museum of Natural History, Los Angeles, California.
Museum of Comparative Zoology, Harvard University, Cambridge, Massachusetts.
Museum of La Plata University, La Plata, Argentina.
Museum of Natural History, Princeton University, Princeton, New Jersey.
National Museum of Natural Sciences, Ottowa, Ontario, Canada.
National Museum of Natural History, Smithsonian Institute, Washington D.C.
Natural History Museum, Mexico City, Mexico.
Peabody Museum of Natural History, Yale University, New Haven, Connecticut.
Provincial Museum of Alberta, Edmonton, Alberta, Canada.
Royal Ontario Museum, Toronto, Ontario, Canada.
Tyrrell Museum of Paleontology, Drumheller, Alberta, Canada.

ASIA
Beijing Natural History Museum, Beijing, China.
Geology Museum, Indian Statistical Institute, Calcutta, India.
Museum of Natural History, Osaka, Japan.
National Science Museum, Tokyo, Japan.
State Central Museum, Ulan-Bator, Mongolia.

AUSTRALIA
Australian Museum, Sydney, New South Wales.
Queensland Museum, Foritude Valley, Queensland.

EUROPE
Bavarian State Collection for Paleontology and Historical Geology, Munich, West Germany.
Central Geological Museum, Leningrad, U.S.S.R.
City Museum and Art Gallery, Bristol, United Kingdom.
Civic Museum of Natural History, Milan, Italy.
Elgin Museum, Elgin, United Kingdom.
Humbold University (Natural History Museum), East Berlin, East Germany.
Institute and Museum of Geology and Paleontology, Tubingen, West Germany.
Institut Royal des Sciences Naturelles de Belgique, Brussels, Belgium.
Musée Nationale d'Histoire Naturelle, Paris, France.
Museum of Paleontology, Institute of Geology, Rome, Italy.
Natural History Museum (British Museum), London, United Kingdom.
Natural History Museum, Vienna, Austria.
Oxford University Museum, Oxford, United Kingdom.
Paleontological Institute, Moscow, U.S.S.R.
Sedgwick Museum (Cambridge University), Cambridge, United Kingdom.
Senckenberg Nature Museum, Frankfurt, West Germany.
Stuttgart Museum, Stuttgart, West Germany.
Royal Scottish Museum, Edinburgh, United Kingdom.

GLOSSARY

Amphibian ("both lives") A four-legged animal that can breathe in water or on land. Living amphibians include frogs and newts.

Aquatic ("water") A plant or animal that lives in water.

Bacteria ("small stick") Simple, microscopic creatures that are made up of single cells.

Biology ("study of life") The science of life and living creatures.

Bipedal ("two-footed") An animal that walks on its hind legs only.

Braincase The part of the skull that contains the brain.

Carapace ("covering") A bony shield covering parts of certain animals, usually the back.

Carboniferous ("coal bearing") The age of coal swamps, from 360 to 286 million years ago when amphibians ruled the earth.

Carnivore ("flesh-eater") A meat-eating animal. The term is often used for cats, dogs, bears, and seals in particular.

Cenozoic ("new life") The period of time from 66 million years ago to today. It is called "new life" because of the many new mammals that evolved during this time. Also known as the Tertiary.

Cheek teeth Teeth in the back of the mouth used for cutting and chewing.

Chemical compound ("chemicals placed together") A substance made up of two or more elements. Water is a chemical compound made from the elements hydrogen and oxygen.

Coal swamp A Carboniferous swamp which, over millions of years, became buried and changed to coal.

Continent ("continuous land") A large land mass. There are seven continents on earth, examples of which are Europe, Africa, and Asia.

Continental drift The movement of the land masses on earth over millions of years.

Cretaceous ("chalk age") The third geological period in the "age of the dinosaurs," the time from 144 to 65 million years ago. Vast layers of chalk were deposited during the Late Cretaceous hence the name "chalk age."

Crust ("shell") The cold surface of the earth which floats on the molten interior.

Cynodont ("dog tooth") Meat-eating mammallike reptiles that include the ancestors of mammals.

Dentine ("tooth") The interior, softer part of a tooth which contains the nerves and blood vessels.

Dinosaur ("terrible lizard") A large land-living reptile of the Triassic, Jurassic, or Cretaceous period.

Enamel ("to coat with") The hard white outer layer of a tooth that covers the softer dentine beneath.

Eocene ("dawning new") The second division of the Cenozoic, a time from 55 to 38 million years ago.

Evolution ("unfolding") The development of plants and animals through geological time, and the way that this development has come about. Animals and plants evolve, or develop, as a result of changes in their living conditions.

Extinct ("wiped out") Animals or plants which lived long ago but have all died out. See *Didus* in the guide.

Fossil ("dug up") The remains of something that once lived. Fossils are often millions of years old, and turned to stone.

Gecko A small lizard found today in warm countries. It can climb walls using its specially shaped toes. The name gecko is an imitation of the sound the animal makes.

Genera ("kinds") A group of very closely related species of plants or animals. We say one *genus*, two *genera*.

Geologist ("earth expert") A scientist who studies rocks and the history of the earth.

Hip girdle A group of bones in the lower back that the hind-limbs attach to. Also known as the pelvic girdle.

Ice age A time, lasting thousands of years, when large parts of the earth were covered by ice.

Ichthyosaur ("fish reptile") Extinct dolphinlike sea reptiles.

Insectivore ("insect-eater") Mammals, like shrews and hedgehogs, that live on insects.

Jurassic ("Jura age": from the Jura mountains where rocks from this period were first named) The second geological period of the "age of the dinosaurs;" the time from 208 to 144 million years ago.

Lagoon A shallow, calm lake connected with the sea or a river.

Limestone A fine-grained sedimentary rock formed from different types of calcium carbonate.

Lizard A small reptile with four legs and a long tail.

Lungfish A fish that can breathe on land because it has a pair of lungs.

Magnetic particle A chemical compound that contains iron and points toward the North Pole.

Mammal A warm-blooded animal with hair that produces milk to feed its young. Examples are mice, rabbits, elephants, and humans.

Mammal-like reptiles A reptile which has some characteristics common to mammals. Mammals evolved from mammal-like reptiles.

Marsupial ("animal with pouch") A mammal which carries its new-born young around in a pouch.

Microscope ("tiny viewer") An optical instrument used to magnify and examine very small things.

Miocene ("less new") The fourth division of the Cenozoic, a time from 25 to 5 million years ago.

Monotreme ("one hole") A primitive mammal which lays eggs instead of giving birth to live young. Examples include the duck-billed platypus and the spiny anteater.

Mudstone A fine-grained sedimentary rock formed from hardened mud.

Multituberculate ("many small humps") A mammal with many bumps and humps on its teeth.

Natural selection A process of nature which removes weak animals, allowing the strongest to survive and breed.

Oligocene ("slightly new") The third division of the Cenozoic, a time from 38 to 25 million years ago.

Order A large group of species that are distantly related to each other — a larger group than a genus or family.

Organism Anything capable of living; all plants and animals are organisms.

Paleocene ("ancient new") The first and oldest division of the Cenozoic. The time from 65 to 55 million years ago when the "new life" of the Cenozoic was just beginning.

Period A division of geological time, such as the Devonian, Permian, or Cretaceous.

Permian ("Perm age": from the Perm district of the U.S.S.R. where rocks from this period were first named) The time from 286 to 248 million years ago when primitive reptiles were abundant.

Placental ("flat cake") A mammal that uses blood vessels to feed its babies as they develop inside the mother's body.

Plate The surface of the earth is split into many sections called plates which move around during continental drift.

Pleistocene ("most new") The sixth division of the Cenozoic, a time from 2 to 0.01 million years ago.

Plesiosaur ("new reptile") Long-necked extinct sea reptile.

Pliocene ("more new") The fifth division of the Cenozoic, a time from 5 to 2 million years ago.

Primate ("one of the first") A placental mammal with a flattened face and very good eyesight. Examples include apes, monkeys, and humans.

Pterosaur ("wing reptile") Ancient flying reptiles, not birds, with wings of skin, not feathers.

Radioactive rock A rock that releases small invisible particles.

Radioactive breakdown The release of small radioactive particles that causes changes in the rock.

Reptile ("crawler") A cold-blooded scaly four-legged animal that lays eggs on land. Living reptiles include snakes, turtles, and crocodiles.

Sail-back A reptile with a large sail or fin on its back that absorbed heat from the sun. See *Dimetrodon* and *Edaphosaurus* in the guide.

Salamander ("tail visible") An amphibian similar in appearance to a newt.

Sandstone A sedimentary rock made from hardened sands deposited in an ancient river, sea, or desert.

Sedimentary rock A kind of rock that was formed from mud or sand, such as sandstone or limestone.

Shoulder girdle A group of bones that the fore-limbs attach to. Also known as the pectoral girdle.

Skeleton The bony framework that holds your body up (and which held up the bodies of all the animals in the guide).

Skull The bones of the head that support the face and protect the brain, eyes, nose, ears, and mouth.

Soft tissue Groups of cells that form all parts of the body except the bones. Soft tissue is usually not preserved in fossils.

Species ("particular kind") A group of animals which all look similar to one another and can breed with one another.

Specimen An example of a plant or animal that a scientist studies.

Subspecies ("part of a species") A group of animals in a species that breed together and look slightly different from the other members of the species.

Symmetrical ("with measure") Something that can be divided into similar, equal portions.

Tertiary ("third division") Another name for the Cenozoic.

Thecodontian ("socket teeth") The first group of reptiles to have their teeth in sockets.

Triassic ("three parts") The first geological period in the "age of the dinosaurs," from 245–208 million years ago. The name "Triassic" refers to the fact that this period is divided into three parts.

Tuatara ("spine on the back") A large reptile found only in New Zealand. It has a row of yellow spines on its back.

Vertebra ("turning joint") A simple bone in the backbone. The backbone is made up of many *vertebrae*.

INDEX

Page numbers in *italics* refer to illustrations.

ACKNOWLEDGMENTS

The publishers would like to thank the following for kindly supplying photographs for this book:

Page 6 Peale Museum, Baltimore; 9 IMITOR; 10 The Mansell Collection *(left)*, The Royal College of Surgeons *(right)*; 14 Photograph by John Reader; 36 Museum of Natural History, Berlin.

Picture Research: Elaine Willis